MEN

Are Like

FISH

What every woman needs to know about catching a man

Steve Nakamoto

JAVA
BOOKS

Huntington Beach, California

Published by Java Books
17202 Corbina Lane, Suite 204
Huntington Beach, California 92649
E-mail: menarelikefish@mindspring.com
Fax: 714-846-0622

Books may be purchased for educational, business, or sales promotional use. For information, please write: Special Marketing, Java Books, 17202 Corbina Lane, Suite 204, Huntington Beach, CA 92649.

Publisher's Cataloging-in-Publication Data
Nakamoto, Steve.
    Men are like fish: what every woman needs to know about
    catching a man /Steve Nakamoto. – Huntington Beach, Calif.:
    Java Books, 2000.
        p. cm.
    ISBN 0-9670893-0-1
        1. Self-help. 2. Relationships. 3. Psychology.
        I. Title.
HG567345.R454345   2000   99-53334
658.9   dc—21   CIP

PROJECT COORDINATION BY JENKINS GROUP, INC.

03 02 01 00 ✿ 5 4 3 2 1

Printed in the United States of America

*Dedicated to helping men and women get and
keep more romantic, exciting, inspiring,
committed, and fulfilling love relationships
through humor and better understanding*

Disclaimer

This book is designed to provide information about the subject matter covered. It is sold with the understanding that the publisher and author are not engaged in rendering any professional services. If expert assistance is required, the services of a competent professional should be sought.

Love relationships are not always easy. Anyone who wishes to succeed must expect to invest a lot of time and effort without any guarantee of success.

Every effort has been made to make this book as complete and accurate as possible. However there may be mistakes, both in typography and in content. Therefore this text should be used only as a general guide and not as the ultimate source of relationship or psychological information.

The purpose of this book is to educate and entertain. The author and publisher shall have neither liability nor responsibility to any person or entity with respect to any loss or damage caused or alleged to be caused directly or indirectly by the information in this book.

If you do not wish to be bound by the above, you may return this book to the publisher for a full refund.

Contents

Contents

Introduction

On Valentine's Day, I went to see the movie, *Message in a Bottle*, starring Kevin Costner, Robin Wright Penn, and Paul Newman. An endorsement for the movie read, "This love story plays the heart like a well-tuned violin."

According to a *Los Angeles Times* story on the Tuesday after that long President's Day weekend, "The romantic drama scored a box-office bull's-eye over the four-day holiday weekend, grossing an estimated $19.1 million in 2,538 theaters."

After seeing the movie, it occurred to me that in spite of many differences, men and women want essentially the same things out of their love lives. They dream of having a love relationship with the following ingredients:

- ⊛ Driving passion
- ⊛ Beautiful romance
- ⊛ Supportive friendship
- ⊛ Spiritual connection
- ⊛ Outrageous fun
- ⊛ Personal growth
- ⊛ Peace of mind

Unfortunately only a few people will ever experience

loving relationships that live up to their dreams. Why is that so?

Most people would say it's just bad luck. But I'm here to say that a lack of results over the course of someone's entire life is more a matter of working an ineffective plan.

For those of you who have tried just about every approach, and still possess the burning desire for a great love life, here's a fresh, new angle on how to capture the heart of a man — an angle that will lead to an exciting, fulfilling, and lasting love relationship.

As a man, I'm certainly not claiming to know how women think and feel. I am also not saying that every woman has to catch a man in order to be happy. Rather, I am offering you a different view of how to make love succeed.

You and I both know that almost everything has already been written on the subject of love and romantic relationships. Therefore you won't find any new information in this book.

What you will find here is a new synthesis that is fun, simple, and easy to understand. Don't be too serious with my approach, otherwise you won't get any mileage out of it. It's only designed as a playful way to quickly master the basics.

> "If you change your perception,
> you'll change your plan,
> and you change your love life."

As you read this book, understand that it is the woman and not the man who holds the ultimate power in a love relationship. Women accomplish this by driving men crazy with desire, keeping them emotionally hooked, and moving their hearts toward the absolute certainty of true love.

When it comes to their approach to finding love, women can be divided into three groups:

- ☙ Those who make things happen
- ☙ Those who wait for things to happen and
- ☙ Those who wonder what happened

This is a book for those women who still have the dream of true love and are willing to make it happen.

CATCH THE LOVE YOU WANT

The major theme of this book is:

> Men are like fish.
> A good one with character, plenty of action, and tons of love to give can be caught by someone like you.

Don't be one of the unfortunate people who misses out on love because of a lack of basic understanding.

Remember the words of Robert Browning, the English poet (1812-1889): "What's the earth with all its art, verse, and music worth...compared with love, found, gained and kept?"

There is no reason to give up on true love. I believe that getting and keeping the man of your dreams is not a complicated process. What every woman needs to know about catching a man is simply that catching a man is like catching a fish.

With this book, you can take what you already know, simplify it, and learn to use it more effectively.

All you need is a willingness to succeed, a fresh start, a dose of your own creativity, and a little help from the other side.

If a fish could talk, this is what he would say on how to catch him and bring him home for keeps.

Men, the fish, are waiting and eager to bite—hook, line, and sinker.

Happy fishing!

A visitor walked into the temple asking questions about Enlightenment.

The Zen Master listened and quietly poured the visitor a cup of tea.

To the visitor's amazement, the Zen Master continued pouring until the cup overflowed and tea spilled all over the table and onto the floor.

The startled visitor asked the Master, "Why are you continuing to fill up my cup after it's already full of tea?"

The Zen Master replied, "I am trying to show you that you are like this tea cup. You are so full of your own preconceived notions that nothing else can go in. I cannot teach you about Enlightenment until you have first emptied out your cup."

The best way to learn to be a fly-fisherman is to go to a river and ask the trout for a few lessons.

Gwen Cooper and Evelyn Haas, Authors
Wade a Little Deeper, Dear (1979)

MEN

Are Like

FISH

IN THE BLEACHERS
By Steve Moore

"I can see swallowing the hook and maybe the line.
But check out the X-ray. This guy's so gullible,
he swallowed the sinker too."

One

The Book

A DIFFERENT ANGLE ON LOVE

And that's what a miracle is:
a parting of the mists, a shift in
perception, a return to love.

Marianne Williamson, Author
A Return to Love: Reflections on the Principles of
A Course in Miracles (1992)

book: 1. a bound volume of written pages encased in protective covers. 2. many years of refined thinking distilled into a condensed written package. 3. the quickest, easiest, and least-painful way to learn about love.

One day as I was flipping through the newspaper, I came across a cartoon strip titled "In the Bleachers" by Steve Moore.

In this cartoon, a fish is talking to another fish saying, "I can see swallowing the hook and maybe the line. But check out the X-ray. This guy's so gullible, he swallowed the sinker too."

A few years ago, I was a gullible guy who fell for a woman, hook, line, and sinker. I chased after the bait of her beauty, got hooked on her personality, and was even caught for a while, only to be thrown back into the waters of single life once again.

> "Love is of all the passions the strongest,
> for it attacks simultaneously the head,
> the heart, and the senses."
> Voltaire, French author

Although it took me a long time to revive myself after that romance, I eventually returned to the dating world eager for more of the same.

As a typical man with fish-like behavior, the mysterious allure of special women is simply irresistible.

Who Catches the Big Ones?

If men are like fish, then women are like fishermen or anglers.

This is a book about how certain women possess the amazing power to "hook" and "land" the attention and hearts of men.

To the surprise of many, the women who possess these magical powers are not necessarily the:

- most beautiful
- most glamorous
- most confident
- most intelligent
- most colorful
- richest
- youngest
- kindest
- best-qualified mate

Instead, the women who end up attracting, capturing, and keeping the attention and hearts of the men they want (the big fish—men who create and contribute consistent, exciting, and lasting happiness) are simply the women who are the most clever at playing the game of love.

Learn to be Clever

Webster's Dictionary defines "clever" as "mentally bright; having sharp or quick intelligence; able, inventive."

Cleverness is the uncanny ability to combine knowl-

If all the good people were clever.
And all clever people were good.
The world would be nicer than ever.
We thought that it possibly could.
But somehow 'tis seldom or never
The two hit it off as they should
The good are so harsh to the clever
The clever, so rude to the good!

Elizabeth Wordsworth
"Good and Clever" (1890) from *Poems and Plays* (1931)

edge, wisdom, skill, creativity, and timing in order to take advantage of opportunities where others don't.

While clever women are catching the big romances, other women have to settle for small love relationships (not very exciting, fulfilling, or lasting) or worse yet, none at all.

But luckily for you, cleverness is not reserved for the privileged few. In this book, I'll show you how cleverness is a learned skill that gets better with study, observation, and practice.

It doesn't take a Ph.D. to write this book. The world is already full of self-help relationship books written by psychologists and professional matchmakers.

> "There's too much information and not
> enough insight and wisdom."
> Mark Victor Hansen, Co-author
> *Chicken Soup for the Soul*

Instead, I offer you a simple, fundamentally sound book from a unique perspective. It is designed to reveal new ideas, while at the same time being easy to understand and remember.

BREAK THE RULES

Unlike any other self-help relationship book that I know of, this book is designed like a tree, from the roots up. Here's what I mean:

The Roots. An American proverb reads: "A man chases a woman until she catches him." This statement serves as the philosophical support of this book. Without the wisdom of this age-old proverb, this book would be nothing more than an unfounded opinion. You will find out more on this in Chapter 2, "The Proverb."

The Tree Trunk. A simple way for me to convey my message is through the use of the metaphor, "Men are like fish." All a woman has to do is learn how to catch a man as an angler would catch a fish. You'll discover more about this in Chapter 3, "The Metaphor."

The Branches. Three main steps in the relationship process include attracting, getting, and keeping the love you want. In fishing terms: attracting is like the bait, getting is like the hook, and keeping is like the net. Other important features, such as beginner's luck, the fish story, fishing line, the big fish, fishing holes, snags, crowds, nibbles, and the strike, form some of the remaining chapters of the book.

The Leaves. Other features of this book include well-researched advice, nationally-syndicated cartoon strips, and wise quotations from writers, philosophers, authors, and experts in the area of love relationships and life. I've sifted through piles of good examples to find a few that I consider most valuable to you.

By following this method, you gain the benefit of good advice that stems from a sound philosophical base.

Get a Fresh Start

The purpose of this book is to entertain and educate. I also hope to inspire you to take a new look at love by removing its mysteries and easing your fears and self-doubts.

No book is the total answer to something as complex as love. But with a little guidance, a different perspective, and some fresh ideas, you can explore your love life with renewed hope.

> "You are never given a wish without also being given the power to make it true."
> Richard Bach, Author
> *Jonathan Livingston Seagull*

An ancient Chinese proverb reads, "A journey of a thousand miles begins with the first step."

You've just taken that first step. Enjoy the rest of the journey!

THE BOTTOM LINE

Don't explore anything or go anywhere without first getting a good guide or a good guidebook. You don't want to lose your way on the journey to love.

Love is like a butterfly which when pursued is just beyond your grasp, but if you will sit down quietly, it may alight upon you.

Nathaniel Hawthorne
American writer (1804-1864)

Two

The Proverb

A MAN CHASES A WOMAN UNTIL SHE CATCHES HIM

Behold the proverbs of a people.

Carl Sandburg,
American author and poet (1878-1967)

prov•erb: 1. a short, witty saying that expresses a truth, fact, or useful idea. 2. aphorism or maxim. 3. a simple principle to put this book on a solid, philosophical foundation.

An American proverb reads, "A man chases a woman until she catches him."

Wolfgang Mieder, the acclaimed "World's Top Proverb Expert" (by *Smithsonian Magazine*) and author of *Illuminating Wit, Inspiring Wisdom: Proverbs From Around the World*, wrote, "Proverbs can be defined as concise traditional statements expressing an apparent truth with currency among the folk. Defined more inclusively, proverbs are short, generally known sentences of the folk which contain wisdom, truths, morals, and traditional views in a metaphorical, fixed, and memorizable form and which are handed down orally from generation to generation."

> "Proverbs are short sayings made out
> of long experiences."
> Zola Neale Hurston, Author
> *Moses: Man of the Mountain*

The proverb, "A man chases a woman until she catches him" contains elements of truth that have been passed down through several generations of Americans. What was true in your great-grandmother's day is largely true even today.

In this book, we will let the long experience of others guide us on the straight and narrow path to love.

THE LOVE PARADOX

"A man chases a woman until she catches him" is an example of a figure of speech called a "paradox." A paradox can be defined as "a seemingly contradictory statement that turns out to be full of truth."

The surprise to many men and women is that our proverb means that the catching is not done by the man (the aggressor) but by the woman instead.

> "A man's desire is for the woman; but the
> woman's desire is rarely other than for
> the desire of the man."
> Samuel Taylor Coleridge, English poet

When the man does the catching, he tends to get restless, starts to wander, and wants to take part in the catching process again.

For most men, the thrill of love lies in the chase. And many men live their entire lives in the pursuit of bigger and grander thrills.

However, when the woman does the catching, a man is more appreciative of a woman's love. He is less likely to wander and more likely to voluntarily take himself out of the singles' dating game for good.

THE MAN DOES THE CHASING

Gelett Burgess, American humorist and author of *Why Men Hate Women* (1866-1951), wrote, "Men like to pursue an elusive woman, like a cake of wet soap in a bathtub; even men who hate baths."

There are really no men at
all. There are grown-up
boys, and middle-aged boys,
and elderly boys, and even
sometimes very old boys.
But the essential difference
is simply exterior. Your man
is always a boy.

Mary Roberts Rinehart, Author
Isn't That Just Like a Man! (1920)

Women who choose to chase men run the risk of going against human nature. Five million years of evolution have produced men as hunters, warriors, conquerors, and more recently, achievers and breadwinners.

To be the object of a woman's desire rather than being the pursuer of a woman may feel instinctively awkward to the average man.

A clever woman understands man's basic nature by attracting a man, while at the same time letting him do the chasing.

If the woman does the chasing, a man is more likely to run in the opposite direction.

THE WOMAN DOES THE CATCHING

Love seems to work better, not when the man is in full control but, when the woman has the man by the proverbial balls.

> "A man has only one escape from his old self:
> to see a different self—in the mirror of
> some woman's eyes."
> Clare Boothe Luce, American journalist

For example, actor Warren Beatty was known as a legendary womanizer. According to the *1999 People Weekly Almanac*, he "broke the hearts of many famous actresses, including Natalie Wood, Leslie Caron, and Joan Collins. Collins even had a wedding dress hanging in a wardrobe for almost a year."

Beatty's wandering days finally ended when actress Annette Benning captured his heart. After that, he married Benning, and by all accounts, lives a happy, married family life.

Beatty recently said, "For me, the highest level of sexual excitement is in a monogamous relationship."

There is no peace of mind for a man until he's the one being caught and not when he's the one who's doing the catching.

Ultimately women have the last word on whether love is going to happen or not.

SOME THINGS NEVER CHANGE

In addition to being filled with useful ideas, this book is founded on sound principles.

> "Principles are the territory. Values are the map. When we value correct principles, we have truth—a knowledge of things as they are."
> Stephen R. Covey, Author
> *The Seven Habits of Highly Effective People*

Principles can be defined as "time-tested rules, laws, guidelines, practices, or methods for effective operation that are based on wisdom or truth." Principles can be either scientific, mathematical, managerial, or psychological in nature.

A clever woman bases her strategy for finding, attracting, getting, keeping, and enjoying the love she wants on the following two organizing principles:

The Man Does the Chasing
&
The Woman Does the Catching

For a woman to do otherwise (chase the man) is more likely to end in failure and frustration than relationship success and happiness.

Helen Rowland, author of *A Guide to Men,* wrote, "A man is like a cat; chase him and he will run. Sit still and ignore him and he'll come purring at your feet."

> "There is only one wisdom: to recognize the intelligence that steers all things."
> **Heraclitus, Byzantine emperor**

Even in today's sophisticated world, some things change slowly, if ever at all. This is especially true when it comes to the game of love that is still played between women and men.

If you want to capture the heart of the man you want, make sure that he does the chasing and pursuing. Your job is to do the catching and persuading.

THE BOTTOM LINE

Nothing is more important to success in life and love than basing your thoughts and actions on timeless, organizing principles.

Three

The Metaphor

MEN ARE LIKE FISH

The greatest thing by far is to be a
master of metaphor. It is the one thing
that cannot be learned from others;
it is also a sign of genius, since
a good metaphor implies
an eye for resemblance.

Aristotle
Ancient Greek philosopher (384-322 B.C.)

met•a•phor: 1. a figure of speech in which a term is applied to something in order to suggest a resemblance. 2. an analogy. 3. a simple way to understand a complex and difficult subject like love.

In the 1994 hit movie, *Forrest Gump*, the central character played by Tom Hanks said, "Life is a box of chocolates." He wasn't describing life literally. He was merely saying that life was like a box of chocolates.

"Life is a box of chocolates" is an example of a metaphor.

University professors George Lakoff and Mark Johnson, in their book titled *Metaphors We Live By*, wrote, "Our ordinary conceptual system, in terms of which we both think and act, is fundamentally metaphorical in nature."

> "All perception of truth is the detection of an analogy."
> Henry David Thoreau, American writer

The word metaphor may sound like an esoteric concept, but in reality, metaphors are a normal part of everyday conversation. Metaphors are nothing more than figures of speech that we use to make complex concepts easier to understand.

MY COURSE IN METAPHORS

In the summer of 1990, I found myself in a conference room at the Maui Marriott Hotel in Hawaii. I was there to be part of the trainer's team for a personal development seminar hosted by peak performance and motivational expert Anthony Robbins.

During his introductory speech to the trainers, Mr. Robbins said, "I've made a lot more distinctions about global metaphors. You all remember what those are? Yes? No? Global metaphors are symbols that we use to represent large areas of our lives."

> "There are many models of life: analogies, allegories, and metaphors to help us understand something as complicated, intricate, and seemingly un-understandable as life."
> Peter McWilliams, Author
> *Life 101*

The seminar taught me how to use effective metaphors to turn complex concepts into simple ideas. Since that time, I've toyed around with the use of metaphors as a new way to understand difficult areas of my life.

One area that needed help was my love life. At the rate I was going, love was going to continue being an irritating source of confusion.

IGNORANCE IS NOT BLISS

Vernon Howard, author of the *Esoteric Mind Power,* wrote, "We are slaves to whatever we don't understand."

The average person may need the equivalent of a bachelor's degree in psychology in order to understand love's complexities. But with the aid of an appropriate metaphor, a person can acquire a good grasp of the subject almost instantly.

The golden light of
metaphor, which is the
intelligence of poetry, was
implicit in alchemical study.
To change, magically, one
substance into another,
more valuable one is the
ancient function of
metaphor, as it
was of alchemy.

Patricia Hampl, Author
A Romantic Education (1981)

As far as love lives are concerned, ignorance is not bliss. More often than not ignorance leads to pain, suffering, regret, and disappointment.

On the other hand, knowledge, wisdom, and understanding are more likely to lead to consistent and lasting success, and happiness in life.

FINDING AN APPROPRIATE METAPHOR

On a visit to a local bookstore, I stumbled across *Well-Cast Lines: The Fisherman's Quotation Book* by John Merwin.

The back cover of Merwin's book quotes Sir John Buchan (1875-1940): "The charm of fishing is that it is a pursuit of what is elusive but attainable, a perpetual series of occasions for hope."

When you think about it, love is a lot like fishing. Consider the following:

- **Love can be very elusive.** The harder you chase it, the less likely you'll get it.
- **Love still seems attainable.** If plenty of average people can have success in their love lives, why can't you and I?
- **Love is a perpetual series of occasions for hope.** Despite our past frustrations and disappointments, we still dream of finding true love.

While fishing may not initially conjure up inspiring images to some women, the sport of fishing is rich in mental value.

Pulitzer Prize winning author James Michener praised

fishing when he said, "The high quality of writing devoted to fishing is a tribute to its value."

John Atherton, author of *The Fly and the Fish* (1950), wrote, "Angling has taught me about art, as art has led to interesting theories and experiments in angling. Thinking and fishing go well together somehow."

In regards to metaphors, fishing and love are a good match. Instead of attracting, getting, and keeping the love you want, you'll learn how to bait, hook, and land him.

WOMEN ARE THE ANGLERS

The next obvious question is this: if love is a lot like fishing, who then is the fisherman and who is the fish?

> "Mark my words, the first woman who fishes for him, hooks him."
> William Makepeace Thackeray, Author
> *Vanity Fair* (1847)

A careful examination of the fishing metaphor pertaining to love leads to an interesting conclusion:

- The fisherman is the one who does the preparation, makes the adjustments, and designs a strategy of action.

- In the area of relationships, women buy 80 percent of books, take the majority of self-improvement courses, and watch the majority of "relationship-oriented" television programs.

- The fish is the one who acts on animal instinct alone.

𝓑 Men who allegedly act like a bunch of animals, don't often seek advice and are not big buyers of relationship or self-help books. Men generally prefer putting their attention on sports, money, work, family, or recreation.

When it comes to the area of love relationships, the weight of the evidence concludes (to the surprise of most men) that men are the fish and women are the fishermen.

MAKE NEW MENTAL CONNECTIONS

Robin Morgan, author of *The Anatomy of Freedom*, wrote, "Metaphor is the energy charge that leaps between images, revealing their connection."

The way to tap into the power of this "men are like fish" metaphor is to make mental connections between catching a fish and catching a man.

> "Since finding out what something is is largely a matter of discovering what it is like, the most impressive contribution to the growth of intelligibility has been made by the application of suggestive metaphors."
>
> Jonathan Miller, Author
> *Images and Understanding* (1990)

While some of the images may be humorous and sometimes outrageous, the value of the metaphor lies in its pure simplicity.

Elizabeth Bowen, the Irish-born English author (1899-1973), wrote, "No object is mysterious. The mystery is the eye."

Making mental connections
is our most crucial learning
tool, the essence of human
intelligence to forge links; to
go beyond the given;
to see patterns,
relationship, context.

Marilyn Ferguson, Author
The Aquarian Conspiracy (1980)

Let the "men are like fish" metaphor open your eyes and take away some of the mystery. Love, which used to be a complex concept, is now easier to understand and remember.

THE BOTTOM LINE

"Men are like fish" is a simple metaphor for understanding what it takes to capture the heart of the one you want. Have fun with it. The more that you play with the metaphor, the more mileage you will get out of it.

BALLARD STREET   Jerry Van Amerongen

Four

Fishing Lessons

IMPROVE YOUR CHANCES
WITH PREPARATION

For the uninitiated, catching fish is a simple business: bait a hook, drop it in the water, see what happens. The seasoned angler knows better. Fish are not caught as they are outsmarted.

Criswell Freeman, Author
The Fisherman's Guide to Life (1996)

fish•ing les•sons: 1. instructions on how to catch more fish. 2. a course in angling knowledge and skill. 3. preparations for attracting, getting, and keeping the love you want.

Top-rated television talk show host Oprah Winfrey (Emmy Award for Best Host of a Talk Show, *The Oprah Winfrey Show,* 1986, 1990, 1991, 1992, 1993, 1994) said, "Luck is a matter of preparation meeting opportunity."

> "One can present people with opportunities.
> One cannot make them equal to them."
> Rosamond Lehmann
> Author of *The Ballad and the Source*

Clever women do not leave their love lives entirely to chance. Instead, they understand that preparation and not luck is the true secret to consistent success at attracting, getting, and keeping the love they want. Examples of love preparation include:

- ⊕ Improving your attitude about love
- ⊕ Enhancing your physical appearance
- ⊕ Refining your communication skills
- ⊕ Developing more self-confidence
- ⊕ Researching good social opportunities
- ⊕ Removing emotional baggage from the past
- ⊕ Facing your fears with courage
- ⊕ Seeking sound relationship advice

There is no denying that luck does play a role in meeting the love you want. But preparation plays a far greater factor when it comes to getting, keeping, developing, and maintaining over the full course of a loving relationship.

Not to think so would be naive.

A SIMPLE FISHING ANALAGY

A typical question to ask a fisherman at the end of a busy day of fishing is, "How was your luck?"

In the sport of fishing, luck is definitely a factor. But the expert angler knows that it is important to separate luck from its far more dominant counterpart, skill.

In *The Complete Idiot's Guide to Fishing Basics*, fishing expert Mike Toth writes: "Only 10 percent of fishermen catch 90 percent of the fish. Many fishermen hit the water with hopes that they'll catch fish, but either they don't consider it a serious pursuit or they don't know enough about the sport itself. The vast majority of these types of fishermen go home empty-handed."

> "Luck enters into every contingency. You are a fool if you forget it — and a greater fool if you count upon it."
> Phyllis Bottome, English-born writer

In today's world, you can improve your chances for success by hiring a fishing guide to teach you how to cast, hook, and land a fish. You can also learn how to read the water for opportunities and what kinds of bait, lures, or flies to use, and when to use them.

In fishing and in your love life, the anglers who rely exclusively on luck usually go home empty-handed. But the smart ones, who take the extra time to study and train, have a much better ratio of success.

DON'T MISS OUT ON LOVE

Not catching any fish may be disappointing to a fisherman, but not experiencing love is far more serious and tragic.

The Danish philosopher and theologian, Soren Kierkegaard (1813-1855), warned, "To cheat oneself out of love is the most terrible deception; it is eternal loss for which there is no reparation either in time or in eternity."

> "When you've missed love, you've missed the essence of life."
>
> Dr. Leo Buscaglia
> Author of *Loving Each Other*

Jim Rohn, author of *Seven Strategies For Wealth and Happiness*, painted a similar picture when he wrote, "It's better to have a love affair in a tent on the beach, than to live in a mansion all by yourself."

Love plays a far too important role in a person's happiness to risk missing out on because of a simple lack of preparation.

PREPARE FOR OPPORTUNITY

To paraphrase Benjamin Disraeli, the English statesman and author (1804-1895), "The secret of success in life is for a woman to be ready for her opportunity when it comes."

In order to help you in this process remember these important points:

- **Keep an open mind.** Great ideas only take root in the minds of those who are ready to receive them. Get ready for new ideas by clearing out the garbage of your old thinking. You can't change your life for the better without first changing your thinking for the better.

- **Expect more out of life.** A Chinese proverb reads, "Raise your sail one foot and you get ten feet of wind." Dare to believe that you deserve better than what your present circumstances show. You rarely get more than you expect. In order to get more out of life, you've got to start expecting to receive more in life.

- **Become a lifelong learner.** Isaac Walton (1593-1683), the father of fly-fishing wrote, "As no man is born an artist, so no man is born an angler." By the same token, no one is born a lover. We all learn about love or fail to learn about love. The lessons of love are constant and never-ending.

- **Start immediately.** A Persian proverb reads, "Go and wake up your luck." Don't procrastinate and hope for the day that love magically appears in your life. Be proactive and make love happen. There are only so many tomorrows.

- **Try new approaches.** Helen Keller, the American writer and lecturer (1880-1968), wrote, "Life is a daring adventure or nothing. Avoiding danger is no safer in the long run than exposure." You are wise in your capacity to experience, not in what you already have experienced. If you continue to do what you've always done, then you will always get what you've always gotten. Be willing to change your approach in order to change your results. The love you want may only be one or two minor adjustments or changes away.

⊗ **Resolve to take full responsibility of your love life.** A Japanese proverb reads, "A firm resolve pierces even a rock." Release everyone, including yourself, from any blame about past relationship failures. The best you can do now is to learn from the past and start on your future. Make a decision to take full responsibility for your new love life. Your pride of ownership will translate into rapid improvements in the quality of your life.

By following these guidelines, you will start turning around your misguided love life and head off in the correct direction toward the love and happiness you want.

PLAY THE PERCENTAGES

Nineteenth-century writer and philosopher, Ralph Waldo Emerson (1803-1882), said, "Shallow men believe in luck. Strong men believe in cause and effect."

Even though Emerson was probably not referring to love when he wrote those words, applying his observation to the context of love is nonetheless valid.

For those of you who remain unconvinced by the

thought of love preparation, the alternative path of neglect was best described by famed college basketball coach, John R. Wooden (the most successful coach in NCAA college basketball history). He wrote, "Failure to prepare certainly means preparing to fail."

> "Love will remain a mystery until you commit yourself to solving the mystery and learn to master the skill of loving."
> Barbara DeAngelis, Ph.D.
> Author of *Making Love All the Time*

If love is something that you truly want in your life, play the percentages wisely by taking the path of preparation, instead of the path of luck. Preparation is the only guaranteed way to consistent, long-term success and happiness in love and life.

THE BOTTOM LINE

Men are like fish. Small ones are easy to catch and require little or no preparation. But big fish are challenging and can only be caught with specialized knowledge, supportive belief, refined skill, and unyielding patience.

Five

Beginner's Luck

RECAPTURE YOUR LOST INNOCENCE

Innocence is a wild trout. But we
humans, being complicated, have to
pursue innocence in complex ways.

Datus Proper, Author
What the Trout Said (1996)

be•gin•ner's luck: 1. the initial success that comes to a person who takes up a new sport. 2. catching a big trout the first time you go fishing is simply "beginner's luck." 3. the good fortune that is attracted to a woman with a fresh, optimistic attitude.

How would you answer the following questions:

- Do you enjoy the company of men?
- Do you like meeting new people?
- How do you feel about the dating process?
- How optimistic are you about falling in love with someone in the not-too-distant future?
- Do you have a lot to contribute to a loving relationship?

What I'm trying to do is help you assess your attitude. Attitude is simply a measure of your level of optimism. It is one of the most important elements to finding, attracting, getting, and keeping the love you want.

> "Attitude determines your altitude."
> Zig Ziglar,
> Author of *See You at the Top*

According to *Mary Kirby's Guide to Meeting Men,* "attitude is simply a way of thinking that translates into action. It's what can make an ordinary-looking woman striking and, by the same token, make a flawless beauty an insipid bore."

50

A SIMPLE FISHING ANALOGY

In the sport of fishing, there is a phenomenon known as "beginner's luck."

Zane Grey, renowned western romance novelist and outdoorsman (1875-1939), wrote, "The preposterous luck of the beginner is well-known to all fishermen. It is an inexplicable thing."

What beginners lack in knowledge and skill, they oftentimes make up for by having great attitudes.

> "There is no aphrodisiac like innocence."
> Jean Baudrillard
> Author of *Cool Memories*

In fishing and in your love life, tap into the inexplicable magic of "beginner's luck" by recapturing and retaining your lost innocence, along with its qualities of youth, vitality, and optimism.

MY FRIDAY NIGHT NETWORKING PARTIES

In Southern California where I live, a woman by the name of Mimi Fane puts on a social networking party every month for so-called "successful eligible singles." All you have to do is get on her mailing list, dress in business attire, and pay ten dollars to get in the door.

Mimi does her best to pack the room with an equal amount of men and women. I know of at least two couples who met at one of Mimi's parties and later married. As a result of these kind of successes, Mimi Fane's parties have a good reputation for meeting quality dating prospects.

Beware of all the paradoxical
in love. It is simplicity which
saves, it is simplicity which
brings happiness.
Love should be love.

Charles Baudelaire
French poet (1821-1867)

What's strange about these networking parties is that everyone knows you're there to meet someone. There's no time wasted trying to qualify someone to see if they are available for dating. At Mimi's parties, everyone is available, including Mimi!

After years of going to these networking socials, my friends and I have come up with the same conclusion: the best prospects are women with the least amount of emotional baggage.

> "Enthusiasm is the divine particle in our composition: with it we are great, generous, and true; without it, we are little, false, and mean."
> L. E. Landon
> Author of *Ethel Churchill*

The lesson to be learned here is: don't scare away prospective men by carrying around a hefty load of bad attitudes.

REJUVENATE YOUR ATTITUDE

While you can't turn back the clock, you can certainly create the same effect by staying young at heart.

With that in mind, here are a few tips for getting and keeping a fresh attitude in your love life:

- **Keep it simple.** Dr. Leo Buscaglia wrote, "Love is very simple; it is we who are complex." Keep your love life simple and your emotions pure. You don't need to know a thousand things to succeed at love. Just master the necessary basics.

- ☙ **Avoid pessimism.** When your experience turns into cynicism, you are essentially finished. Don't let your past hurts accumulate and sour your attitude. They will only ruin your chances for love.

- ☙ **Put your trust back into love.** Believe that "all things happen for a reason and a purpose and it serves you." Regardless of past disappointments, put your faith back into love. Your success and happiness depend on how optimistic you are about love, life, and yourself.

- ☙ **Surrender your ego.** Sometimes in order for love to work, you have to forget about yourself and get involved in life. Be willing to let the chips fall where they may. Realize that part of love is out of your immediate control. In order to find love, you have to be willing to let go of the controls.

- ☙ **Forget parts of your past.** Sometimes it is necessary to turn your attention completely away from the past. Both good and bad memories, too well remembered, can prevent you from enjoying present happiness to its fullest.

- ☙ **Let love surprise you once again.** Just when you think you have love figured out, something will come along and bring you back to your knees. That's a good thing, however. For some unexplainable reason, part of love will always remain mysterious and magical. Don't try to figure love out. Let love surprise you once again and learn how to enjoy the ride.

If you follow these guidelines, you will rejuvenate your attitude and revitalize your love life.

YOUR RETURN TO LOVE

Some women may say, "I'm too experienced to be innocent again."

All I can say is take heart in the words of American writer James Baldwin (1924-1987). They worked wonders for me: "Experience, which destroys innocence, also leads one back to it."

Stay fascinated in love. Study and learn all you can, but keep a healthy respect for love's magic. Love has a funny habit of being wooed by a person's innocence instead of their experience.

> "Youth is a quality, and if you have it,
> you never lose it."
> Frank Lloyd Wright,
> American architect

Return to love with the expectation of great things and you can tap into the "inexplicable luck of the beginner."

A young heart never grows old.

THE BOTTOM LINE

Beginner's luck comes to those who expect only the best. You can change your love life for the better, by first changing your attitude for the better. Good results naturally follow good attitudes.

SINGLE SLICES   by Peter Kohlsaat

Six

The Fish Story

LET GO OF THE BIG ONE THAT GOT AWAY

In every species of fish I've angled for, it is the ones that have got away that thrilled me the most, the ones that keep fresh in my memory. So I say it is good to lose fish.

Ray Bergman
Author of *Trout* (1949)

fish sto•ry: 1. an implausible, boastful, incredible story owing to the fact that fishermen tend to exaggerate the size of their catch. 2. a lost love affair that you can't easily forget. 3. your excuse for living in the past instead of the present.

Some people are hard to forget, especially the ones who leave you with a broken heart.

English poet laureate, William Wordsworth (1770-1850), wrote, "Though nothing can bring back the hour of splendor in the grass, or glory in the flower; we will grieve not, rather find strength in what lies behind."

While some people may think it is romantic to reflect back on past romances, it's an entirely different beast when those same memories prevent them from present and future happiness.

A SIMPLE FISHING ANALOGY

In fishing terminology, a "fish story" is a boastful tale about how the big fish escaped capture. The common occurrence is for the angler to greatly exaggerate the size of the fish that was initially hooked and later managed to escape.

Some interesting insights that can be drawn from "fish stories" include:

- ⑨ Nothing grows faster than a fish from the time he bites until the time he gets away.
- ⑨ A fish is larger for being lost. (Japanese proverb)

- There is a critical difference between "hooking" a fish and actually "landing" it.
- The fish that escaped is the big one. (Chinese proverb)
- All anglers have a fish in their memory that still haunts them.

In fishing and in your love life, remember that the thrills of the big ones that got away always seem better than they actually were.

A BIG ONE THAT GOT AWAY

Stories of lost love happen to both men and women. Here's my reference of how painful it feels from a man's perspective.

A few years ago, I found myself working in a new career as a professional tour director. At the time I was traveling with a busload of senior citizens on a tour called, "Autumn in New England."

> "A long past vividly remembered is like
> a heavy garment that clings to your limbs
> when you would run."
>
> Mary Antin
> Author of *The Promised Land*

We were driving by beautiful fall foliage along the Mohawk Trail in central Massachusetts. The shadows at that time of year, the color of the leaves, and the smell of autumn in the air reminded me of my trip to see a woman I dearly loved years ago.

It is our lost fish that I believe stay longest in our memory, and seize upon our thoughts whenever we look back to fishing days. The most gallant fish when eaten is forgotten, but the fish that, after a mad glorious battle, has beaten us and left us quivering with excitement and vexation, is hooked and lost again in many years to come.

A.H. Chayton
Author of *A Letter to a Salmon Fisher's Son*
from
The Angler's Quotation Book by Eric Restall

A passenger in the front row of the bus asks me, "Steve, you seem to know a lot about the area. How many times have you been to New England?"

I reply, "I've only been here a few times. The first time was to visit a woman that I really liked. We had one of those 'Love Boat' romances many years ago."

"Hey, Steve, whatever happened to her?" asks another passenger.

I answer, "She's still around. And everything is just fine between us. There is, however, a slight problem. You see she lives in Connecticut and I live in California. She also happens to be married to a guy named Paul. And she has two young sons. Aside from that, things couldn't be better."

Many of the passengers laughed. Others looked at me with pity. In spite of my joking around and the passing of several years, my sadness of lost love must have showed.

Although I'll probably never forget that romance, I've been able to move ahead in my life with the help of a fishing perspective.

LET GO OF THE PAST

If you have a "fish story" that is getting in your way of present and future happiness, here are ways to complete your past:

- **Find a moral to your story.** Close out that chapter of your life by putting an empowering final lesson to your fish story. And then turn the page.

- **Focus on the love life in front of you.** A French proverb reads, "New love drives out old love." Like when you are driving a car, you must quit looking in the rear view mirror and keep your eyes peeled on the new love that is about to appear in front of you.

⊛ **Think abundance not scarcity.** An old saying goes, "There are plenty of fish in the sea." Realize that it only takes one fish in the sport of love. If you maximize your opportunities, there will be plenty for you to choose from.

⊛ **Take bold steps.** A German proverb reads, "Boldly ventured is half won." If it becomes necessary, get rid of all the old cards and love letters, turn off the love songs, and remove other unwanted reminders that keep you glued to a time that will never return.

⊛ **Outgrow your past.** A lost love from sixth grade shouldn't hurt too much when you graduate from college. That's because you're not the same person when you graduate from college as you were in sixth grade. Use the same principle in your adult life in order to outgrow your past loves.

⊛ **Never look back.** It's tough to eliminate the past. But if the mere thought of the past brings up consistent regret and loss, then take one last look and never look back.

Follow these steps and you will leave the past where it belongs—behind you.

Move Forward

The final step to letting go of the big one that got away is to move forward.

Remember these words of wisdom from Benjamin Disraeli, English prime minister and statesman (1804-1881): "The magic of first love is our ignorance that it can never end."

Never remain stuck in your love life. Keep moving forward in the direction of new love until you get it right.

> "Don't limit yourself to the idea of one life—one love. Plan to have at least four important loves in your life."
>
> Sally Jessy Raphael
> Author of *Finding Love*

For love to happen again, you must complete your relationship "fish stories." Let go of the big ones that got away, learn from your mistakes, and turn the page to the present. The love of your life is ahead of you, not behind.

The Bottom Line

Men are like fish. Once you lose them, they are almost impossible to catch with the same bait again. Play it smart by moving ahead to your next love opportunity.

I know there are nights when I have power, when I could put on something and walk in somewhere, and if there is a man who doesn't look at me, it's because he's gay.

Kathleen Turner, American Actress
from *An Uncommon Scold* by Abby Adams

Seven

The Fishing Rod

GET A FIRM GRIP
ON YOUR SELF-CONFIDENCE

Confidence—the single most
important item an angler needs.
Without this essential requirement,
many fish otherwise taken,
will be lost.

Peter Lightfoot and Kevin Whay
Authors of *Stillwater Trout Fly-Fishers' Ready Reference*
from *The Angler's Quotation Book* by Eric Restall

fish•ing rod: 1. a long, slender pole made out of wood, steel, or fiberglass for use with a reel in catching fish. 2. the main piece of equipment in fishing. 3. a woman's self-confidence.

Samuel Johnson, the English author (1715-1774), wrote, "Self-confidence is the first requisite to great undertakings."

All the knowledge in the world is of little value without following through by taking outstanding actions. And nothing takes away from the quality of a person's actions more than an abundance of self-doubt.

> "You've got to take the initiative and play your game. In a decisive set, confidence is the difference."
>
> Chris Evert
> Tennis champion

Before you start expanding your knowledge and improving your skills for attracting, getting, and keeping love, make sure you solidify your base of self-confidence.

A SIMPLE FISHING ANALAGY

A visit to the fishing department of a sporting goods store will put you in front of all sorts of equipment. You will find a variety of items such as bait, lines, hooks, sinkers, fishing rods, reels, nets, and lures. From this selection, the first item that a novice should buy is a fishing rod.

According to *Fishing For Dummies* by Peter Kaminsky, "The rod is the symbol of the angler in the same way that a gun is the symbol of the hunter. Just as you need a bullet or shell to shoot an animal, you need a reel and a line to catch a fish. But the rod, like the gun, is the main ingredient."

In fishing and in your love life, it is critical to determine what is the main ingredient to your success and start building from there.

CONFIDENCE CAN BE LEARNED

A few years ago, I went to the Club Med village at Sonora Bay, Mexico. One of the people vacationing there was a fascinating young woman from San Francisco named Angela.

All the men (and women) at Club Med couldn't help but notice Angela. Besides being stunningly attractive, she also radiated an air of absolute self-confidence.

> "Sex appeal is 50% what you've got and 50% what people think you've got."
> Sophia Loren
> Italian-born actress

One afternoon on the water-ski dock, I got a chance to talk with Angela. I discovered that she was a professional model. She said that her training for modeling included learning how to dress, how to groom, how to walk, and how to handle herself with poise.

Angela's training paid off big the following year, when she became a *Playboy* Playmate of the Month.

GET A FIRM GRIP ON YOUR CONFIDENCE

To help you increase your self-confidence, here are some pointers for more rapid improvements:

- ☞ **Start by being kind to yourself.** A Yiddish proverb reads, "Do not make yourself low; people will tread on your head." Be your own best supporter instead of the leading critic. Listen to how you talk to yourself. If you don't like what you hear, change it immediately. You can't rise to the top if you're constantly tearing yourself down.

- ☞ **Stop comparing yourself with others.** Doubt usually comes from comparing yourself with others who are superior to you in some narrow context. All people have both strengths and weaknesses. Refuse to play the comparison game. You'll either destroy yourself or destroy others along the way. Neither are good for your psyche.

- ☞ **Narrow your focus.** You can't be masterful at everything, but there are a few areas that you can be real good at. Find your areas of strength and build your confidence around these. Handle your weaknesses but move ahead with your strengths.

- ☞ **Change the words you use.** Begin using words and phrases that demonstrate more confidence and less doubt. Become more decisive on what things mean to you and then communicate your message with more clarity and certainty.

- ☞ **Strengthen your voice.** Pay more attention to how you sound in terms of confidence. Observe the voice tones of successful media or entertainment celebrities. Follow their examples by speaking with more vocal power by adjusting your volume, tone, pitch, and rhythm.

🅥 **Move your body with more certainty.** Nothing communicates how you feel about yourself more than the way you move and hold your body. Demonstrate more confidence in the way you walk, gesture, breathe, stand, make facial expressions, and create muscle tension.

🅥 **Get in excellent physical shape.** A healthy diet, vigorous exercise, and plenty of rest can do wonders for strengthening your mind, body, and spirit. You can't rise to meet your challenges in life if your body is constantly letting you down.

🅥 **Cultivate boldness.** A French proverb reads, "The bashful always lose." Take chances and live with no regrets. There is nothing to lose except lost opportunities. Be bold and take decisive actions often.

When you possess solid confidence in yourself, you enjoy the freedom to go into any situation and perform with effectiveness, elegance, and absolute certainty.

LOVE YOURSELF FIRST

While you're going through the confidence building process, remember the words of actress-comedian Lucille Ball (1911-1989), "I have an everyday religion that works for me. Love yourself first and everything else falls into line.

There's a magnificence in you, Tracy ... a magnificence that comes out of your eyes and your voice and the way you stand and the way you walk. You're lit from within, Tracy. You've got fires banked in you, hearth fires and holocausts.

James Stewart to Katharine Hepburn
The movie: *The Philadelphia Story*
from
Screen Kisses by Ian Hardy and Gretchen Zufall

You really have to love yourself to get anything done in this world."

> "Just love and accept yourself, and express the
> truth of who you are in the moment."
>
> Jack Canfield
> Co-author of *Chicken Soup for the Soul*

Self-confidence is nothing more than trusting and accepting yourself. For many people this is a slow building process. But for others, confidence begins the instant they decide to simply love themselves unconditionally.

For others to love you, remember that you must first love yourself.

THE BOTTOM LINE

The quality of your actions are either increased or reduced by how you feel about yourself. Start your new love life by getting a firm grip on your self-confidence. It is the main ingredient to your success and happiness at love.

Quality Time

by Gail Machlis

Eight

The Bait

MAKE YOUR ATTRACTION MORE POWERFUL

You cannot bring a hook into a fish's
mouth unless there is food on it
that pleases him.

Dame Juliana Berners
Author of *Treatise of Fishing with an Angle* (1450)
from
Well-Cast Lines by John Merwin

bait: 1. a piece of food that is used to entice or lure a fish. 2. the qualities of women that attract men. 3. the first skill of love.

An American proverb reads, "A man chases a woman until she catches him." What that means to a woman is: if a man doesn't chase you, then there is no chance of catching him.

The force that causes a man to chase is something called "attraction." Attraction works like a magnet. The more powerful the magnet, the more it will attract.

Jim Rohn, author of *Seven Strategies For Wealth and Happiness,* wrote, "To attract attractive people, you first must be attractive. Go to work on yourself. If you become, you can attract."

If you want a wide range of quality men to choose from, then you'd better make your attraction as powerful as you possibly can.

A Simple Fishing Analogy

In the sport of fishing, bait is used to attract a fish to the angler's fishing line.

The label on a jar of a product called *Power Bait* reads, "Fish Bite and Won't Let Go! *Berkeley Power Bait* contains advanced scent and flavor that dispenses to attract trout, salmon, and steelhead. Firmly cover the hook with floating Trout Bait for best results."

Bait is one of the secrets to successful fishing. Fishing experts say that catching fish can be absurdly easy if you use the right bait.

In fishing and in love, the bait you use determines how powerfully you can attract what you want to catch.

THE BEAUTIFUL WOMAN SYNDROME

At a beach party this past summer, I overheard a conversation between two young women. It went something like this:

> "Why doesn't Johnny ask me out?" asked a slightly overweight woman in a much-too-tight red dress.
>
> "It's because of the beautiful woman syndrome," replied her friend.
>
> "What's that?" asked the first.
>
> "That's when a woman is so beautiful a guy is too intimidated to ask her out. That's what you've got going with Johnny. You're so beautiful he's too scared to ask you out."

I had to laugh at first, but then again there is some truth to the beautiful woman syndrome. Unless you're model Cindy Crawford, you'll need more than just a pretty face to attract the man you want.

MASTER THE BASICS

If you read all the women's magazines and all the books in the area of love relationships, you would probably come up with hundreds, if not thousands, of useful tips on how to become a more attractive woman.

But knowing hundreds of ideas may not translate into immediate success. More often than not, too much information leads to confusion rather than to certainty and peak performance.

> "Bait is a preparation that renders the hook more palatable. The best kind is beauty."
>
> Ambrose Bierce
> American author

The smart strategy is to concentrate the bulk of your time and energy on the few key areas that make the greatest difference in your love life.

Wynn Davis, author of *The Best of Success: A Treasury of Success Ideas*, wrote: "Concentration is the magic key that opens the door to accomplishment. By concentrating our efforts upon a few major goals, our efficiency soars, our projects are completed—-we are going somewhere. By focusing our efforts to a single point, we achieve the greatest results."

Mental focus is one of the secrets to rapid personal development.

MAKE YOUR ATTRACTION MORE POWERFUL

Remember that the woman with the most powerful attraction has a decisive advantage over her competition. With that in mind, here are five primary areas of attraction to concentrate your major energies on:

- **Keep your bait fresh.** If you were the Homecoming Queen of Rolling Hills High School in 1971, it's time to get over it and move on to the new you.

Update your personal references by reinventing yourself into the best possible package for today. There's nothing worse than having to watch a tired act. Keep your bait fresh and stay current with your love life of today.

⊛ **Maximize your physical talents.** Do all you can in terms of improving and refining your beauty, attire, health, fitness, vitality, voice quality, and physical movements. The woman who looks outstanding, sounds alluring, touches with warmth, and is stunning to watch in action gets the initial and consistent attention of men.

⊛ **Develop your game.** An Irish proverb reads, "Beauty will not make the pot boil." What does make a man boil is a woman who knows how to play the game of love. Find ways to increase your ability to communicate, entertain, and persuade effectively. The most attractive women are those who can move men emotionally, not intellectually. The woman with the most game creates the most intrigue.

⊛ **Play with more heart.** A Philippine proverb reads, "Beauty will fade, but not goodness." Demonstrate your emotional range in terms of desire, warmth, compassion, gratitude, joy, sincerity, tolerance, understanding, sensitivity, generosity, and flexibility. Beware of deductions that are made out of anger, criticism, jealousy, bitterness, or cynicism. Quality men will do their most critical measuring around the heart of a woman.

Charm... it's a sort of bloom
on a woman. If you have it,
you don't need to have
anything else; and if you
don't have it, it doesn't
much matter what else
you have.

James M. Barrie
Author of *What Every Woman Knows* (1997)

⑨ **Move up in class.** In the sport of horse racing, the winner is usually not the fastest horse but the one with the most class. Class determines how much strength remains for the critical challenge of the final stretch. Go to work on refining your elements of poise, elegance, command, taste, grace, charm, and style. These qualities will stand out when the going gets tough and push you ahead of the pack.

It doesn't take a thousand minor things to be successful in any phase of life. It only takes the mastery of the basics.

FIND A GOOD COACH

Ann Landers, nationally syndicated columnist, advised, "Don't accept your dog's admiration as conclusive evidence that you are wonderful."

> "Women look for talent, men for beauty."
> Vietnamese proverb

Attraction is a major part of the love game. In order to play the game to win, be sure to find yourself a good coach who has your best interests at heart.

When the competition gets tough, clever people get good advice and feedback. That's true in sports, business, life, and love.

One piece of important advice in a critical area of your love life may be all you need. It could be something like remedying bad breath, changing your hairstyle, speaking with more confidence, learning how to listen, being more

Men Are Like Fish

Advice for a teenage daughter—five inexpensive beauty hints:

For attractive lips, speak words of kindness.

For lovely eyes, seek out the good in people.

For a slim figure, share your food with the hungry.

For beautiful hair, let a child run his fingers through it once a day.

And for poise, walk with the knowledge that you will never walk alone.

Sam Levenson
American humorist and author (1911-1980)

approachable, going out to new places, or dating men who are better suited for you.

Find someone you can trust and ask them for help. At first, be sure to brace yourself for the feedback. Then ask for solutions, make adjustments and eventually reap the benefits.

> "Advice is what we ask for when we already know the answer but wish we didn't."
> Erica Jong
> Author of *How to Save Your Own Life*

Remember that the greatest number of love choices usually go to the women who possess the most powerful ability to attract.

Before you go looking for love, make sure your bait is absolutely irresistible.

THE BOTTOM LINE

Men are like fish. You can only catch the ones who chase after your bait. The most attractive and available bait always receives the first serious look.

SINGLE SLICES

by Peter Kohlsaat

Nine

The Fishing Line

TAKE UP THE SLACK IN YOUR SMALL TALK

If there is a lot of slack line, the fish will
be able to shake his head to throw out
the hook. Slack line will almost
always cause trouble.

Cathy Beck
Author of *Cathy Beck's Fly-Fishing Handbook* (1996)

fish•ing line: 1. a string, usually made out of monofilament plastic, that is used to catch fish. 2. the connection or bond between the angler and the hook. 3. casual conversation or small talk.

What you say and how you say it can either help or hurt your chances for love.

Oscar Wilde, Irish playwright and wit (1854-1900), said, "Ultimately, the bond of all companionship, whether marriage or friendship, is conversation."

> "Each person's life is lived as a series of conversations."
>
> Deborah Tannen
> Author of *You Just Don't Understand*

If you want to maintain a strong bond with a prospective romance, be sure you acquire and maintain good conversational skills.

A SIMPLE FISHING ANALOGY

In the sport of fishing, the fishing line is what connects the angler with the fish. When a fish falls off the hook, it is often the result of too much slack in the line.

Slack line is the result of carelessness and neglect.

In order to prevent this unfortunate event from happening, maintain a tight, responsive connection with your catch, by taking up all the unnecessary slack in your line.

That applies to both fishing and your love life.

MY SINGLES' DINING CLUB

A few years ago in the hope of expanding my social life, I bought a membership in a singles' dining club called "A Table For Six." For an additional cost of fifteen dollars plus the price of dinner, I got the chance to dine at a nice local restaurant with three single women and two other single men.

One of the most obvious things that stood out in this social situation was how well or how poorly people were at conversational small talk.

> "Conversation is like a dear little baby that is brought in to be handed round. You must rock it, nurse it, keep it on the move if you want it to keep smiling."
> Katherine Mansfield
> Author of *The Doves' Nest*

For example, some friendly discussions escalated into heated debates. Other times conversations veered off into sensitive subjects, like religion, abortion, politics, sex, and money. And still other conversations were simply boring.

"A Table For Six" was like a conversational appetizer. If you liked the taste of the appetizer, then you were likely to dig into more of the same.

But as many of us in the club discovered, after one dining experience with a poor conversationalist we had more than our fill.

IMPROVE YOUR COMMUNICATION SKILLS

The quality of your relationship with another person is

The conversation of two
people remembering, if the
memory is enjoyable to
both, rocks on like music or
lovemaking. There is a
rhythm and a predictability
to it that each anticipates
and relishes.

Jessamyn West
Author of *The State of Stony Lonesome* (1984)

no better than the quality of your communication skills. Unfortunately few people ever take the time to examine how well they converse.

Oliver Wendell Holmes, American physician and author (1809-1894), pointed out, "Talking is one of the fine arts, the noblest, the most important, and the most difficult."

For improved communications, here are a few valuable pointers that will serve you well in taking up the slack in your small talk:

☘ **Be brief.** Mark Twain once wrote, "The worst kind of death is to be talked to death." Don't bore people with long monologues. Learn to say what you have to say quickly, get to the point, and let the other person have a chance to talk.

☘ **Watch your audience closely.** Keep your audience awake and involved in your small talk. Also learn to distinguish between courtesy and genuine interest. If your audience starts to fidget, it probably means that they are not listening to you. That's your cue to stop talking and start listening.

☘ **Have something good to say.** Find ways to increase your range of interesting topics by either study or experience. Learn to broaden your horizons day to day and week to week so you will have something of interest to talk about. Stay current by reading a daily newspaper like the *USA Today.*

☘ **Learn the art of saying it well.** Become more adept at the regular use of candor, humor, sincerity, and enthusiasm. Learn to tell a story that is fresh, colorful, enjoyable, and alive. Talking has a lot more to do with how well you say things rather than the actual words you say. A good conversationalist can make even the mundane sound extraordinary.

◎ **Learn what not to say.** Dorothy Neville, author of *Under Five Reigns* (1910), wrote, "The real art of conversation is not only to say the right thing in the right place, but, far more difficult still, to leave unsaid the wrong thing at the tempting moment." Sometimes in our quest for lively conversation we have to choose between what is honest, what is advantageous, and what is better off being left unsaid. Each option has its appropriate moment.

◎ **Back your words with emotion.** Be sure to reinforce your small talk with the power of your emotions. People are more impressed and moved by how you feel than by what you know. Express with emotion and you can impress with impact.

A German proverb reads, "Practice makes the master." No matter where you are now in terms of your present skill, you will become effective at communications with practice and effort.

Judge By Response

The final point to remember is that the quality of your communications is not determined by how eloquent you think you sound. Instead the quality of your communication skills is judged by the quality of the response you get.

Samuel Johnson, the British author (1709-1784), observed, "The happiest conversation is that of which nothing is distinctly remembered but a general effect of pleasing impression."

The best-crafted speech and the noblest of intents are of little value if your target audience reacts in a negative way.

> "Too much brilliance has its disadvantages, and misplaced wit may raise a laugh, but often beheads a topic of profound interest."
> Margot Asquith
> Author of *More or Less About Myself*

A woman who keeps a man fascinated and hungry for more connection, has done a great job of taking up the slack in her line.

THE BOTTOM LINE

Men are like fish. Remember to take up the slack in your small talk so that you maintain a good connection with your prospective catch. Otherwise, a man will fall off the hook because of declining interest.

Ten

The Hook

USE ONLY THE MOST SECURE DEVICES

People become emotionally "hooked"
on those persons who can truly satisfy
their never-ending need
for human understanding.

Thomas McKnight and Robert Phillips
Authors of *Love Tactics: How to Win the Love You Want*
(1988)

hook: 1. a curved or sharply bent piece of metal used to catch fish. 2. a capturing device that is disguised by bait. 3. the key elements that secure a man to a woman.

A loving relationship is in trouble the minute a man starts losing interest in a woman. With this awareness, a clever woman makes sure that her man's attention is firmly secured. There are two ways to accomplish this. One way is by tricking a man with deception and manipulation. The other is by filling a man's deepest needs, quickly and elegantly.

Both methods can work very well in the short term. But the latter is the more secure, dependable, and lasting approach.

If you want to secure your love for the long-term, stick with consistently filling a man's deepest needs.

A SIMPLE FISHING ANALOGY

In the sport of fishing, the device that keeps the fish on the line is called a hook or fishhook.

This fall, I took a trip to Springfield, Missouri to visit the largest sporting goods store in America called *The Bass Pro Shop*. While I was there, I discovered that fishhooks come in various shapes, sizes, and qualities. Fishhooks can be barbed, treble, snelled, long shank, open bend, clawbeak, weedless, and salmon egg hooks, to name a few.

A Japanese company now makes a hot-selling brand of fishhooks that are seven times sharper and four times stronger than average ones. These high-quality hooks help prevent fish from falling off during the difficult landing process.

Gene Kugach, author of *Fishing Basics: The Complete Illustrated Guide*, wrote, "The most important thing to remember when buying hooks is to look for hooks made by a reputable manufacturer. Cheap hooks lose fish."

For consistent success in fishing and in your love life, use only the highest quality and most secure hooking devices.

THE HIGHEST QUALITY HOOK

There is no denying that outstanding beauty is one of the most obvious ways to "hook" a man.

But beauty alone does not secure love. Otherwise, the rate of failed relationships would not be so historically high among Hollywood celebrities.

> "Love built on beauty, soon as beauty, dies."
> John Donne
> English poet

William James, American psychologist and philosopher (1842-1910), suggested that rather than desire for beauty, "The deepest principle in human nature is their craving to be appreciated."

By learning the art of sincere appreciation, a person can better secure a lasting relationship. Three sensitive areas to look at when you appreciate a man include:

- ⚘ **Respect.** Appreciate a man for his knowledge, dexterity, expertise, command, control, dominance, power, accomplishments, position, or

They used to say that the fastest way to a man's heart was through his stomach. Now we know better. The fastest and surest way to a man's heart is through his ego. This is the most sensitive part of a man, the part that responds most enthusiastically to a woman's interest.

Mary Kirby
Author of *Mary Kirby's Guide to Men* (1983)

prestige. Men who pride themselves on achievement respond well to recognition.

- ☺ **Like.** Appreciate a man for his sense of humor, wit, personality, and personal charm. Men who pride themselves as being "people persons" respond well to being liked by others.

- ☺ **Attractiveness.** Appreciate a man for his physical beauty, fitness, strength, and taste in clothes. Men like to be physically attractive to women.

Men and women alike respond well to appreciation. It is a basic principle in human nature.

USE GOOD LISTENING SKILLS

Dr. Joyce Brothers, psychologist and author, wrote, "Listening, not imitation, may be the sincerest form of flattery.... If you want to influence someone, listen to what he says."

> "Men aren't attracted to me by my mind.
> They're attracted by what I don't mind."
> Gypsy Rose Lee
> American actress

Listening is the most basic form of sincere appreciation. Here are seven suggestions for making your listening more effective:

- ☺ **Show sincere interest.** Search for and find something fascinating, enjoyable, agreeable, or interesting in what a man has to say. A man is often impressed more by what a woman listens to rather than what she says.

⊛ **Ask a thought-provoking question.** Search for deeper meaning or clarification by asking a thought-provoking question. If you can, ask questions that elicit good feelings that empower the man.

⊛ **Give a highly-valued compliment.** Find something positive about a character trait or the good tastes of a man. Men are especially disarmed by a timely and sincere compliment.

⊛ **Pause before replying.** Give extra value to what a man has to say by pausing briefly before replying. Pausing is classy. It demonstrates respect for what a man has to say.

⊛ **Reinforce with candor.** Never underestimate the power of candor. You can score a direct hit to the heart of a man by using the bold honesty of candor when the appropriate moment arises.

⊛ **Perceive rather than judge.** Get in the habit of seeing things from the man's point of view. Getting perturbed about what a man says only shuts off his willingness to be open. At the same time, he may also shut off his heart to you.

Practice and perfect your listening skills and you will show appreciation in the most basic and subtle way.

KEEP YOUR HOOKS SHARP

A woman's goal is to persuade the man she is interested in that he is deeply appreciated, now and forever.

The degree to which a woman can consistently, creatively, and elegantly appreciate a man in the sensitive areas of his life will determine the quality and strength of her hook.

> "What do we call love, hate, charity, revenge, humanity, magnanimity, forgiveness? Different results on the one Master Impulse: The necessity of securing one's self-approval."
>
> Mark Twain
> American writer

If you use the highest-quality hooks, you can withstand the inevitable cross-currents of adversity that hit all love relationship.

Cheap hooks lose fish.

Quality hooks keep love secure.

THE BOTTOM LINE

Men are like fish. The big ones put up a good fight in order to avoid being caught. Use only the highest quality hooks to insure that the love you want doesn't escape.

Quality Time   by Gail Machlis

Eleven

The Big Fish

DECIDE EXACTLY WHAT YOU WANT TO CATCH

The fish is not so much your quarry as
your partner.

Arnold Gingrich
Author of *The Well-Tempered Angler* (1965)

big fish: 1. what every angler dreams of catching. 2. a man who contributes tons of pleasure and very little pain to a relationship. 3. the perfect love match for you.

Over the years, the widespread popularity of motion pictures like *Doctor Zhivago, Gone With the Wind, Romeo and Juliet, The Way We Were, Sleepless in Seattle, The Bridges of Madison County, Titanic,* and *Shakespeare in Love* have shown how much women dream of having a beautiful romance with a special kind of man.

But that brings up an interesting question: what exactly would it take for a man to be special to you?

The Sexiest Man Alive Award

Every year *People Magazine* comes out with an issue that is titled "The Sexiest Man Alive." Past honorees include Mel Gibson, Mark Harmon, Harry Hamlin, John F. Kennedy, Jr., Sean Connery, Tom Cruise, Patrick Swayze, Nick Nolte, Brad Pitt, Denzel Washington, and George Clooney. The 1998 honor went to actor Harrison Ford of *Star Wars* and *Indiana Jones* fame.

If any man would be considered a "big catch" to women, it would be Harrison Ford. His unique blend of good looks, personality, fame, and success makes him one of the most adored men in the world in the eyes of women.

Harrison Ford seems to have it all. As a woman looking for a great relationship, rather than a mediocre one, you also want to find a man who has it all—that is, all the ingredients necessary to create a great love relationship with you.

A SIMPLE FISHING ANALOGY

In fishing the novice angler dreams of catching the biggest fish or the largest number of fish. But veteran anglers think differently.

Tom Davis, author of *The Little Book of Fly Fishing*, wrote, "The Basic Truths: The dimension of the reward is proportional to the size of the challenge, not the size of the fish. You've heard it before, but it's true—as anyone who's snaked a ten-incher out of an impossible spot will emphatically attest."

In fishing and in your love life, the size of the reward is proportional to the size of the important intangibles. Your ability to identify and measure these intangibles becomes the secret to finding the "big one" for you.

THE BIG FISH EQUATION

Voltaire, the French writer (1694-1778), wrote, "Pleasure is the object, the duty, the goal of all rational creatures."

> "Everything you and I do, we do either out of our need to avoid pain or our desire to gain pleasure."
> Anthony Robbins
> Author of *Awaken the Giant Within*

On the other hand, an American proverb reminds us to "Always count the cost."

A wise person must both recognize this desire to seek pleasure, and remember to weigh the costs.

For simplicity, the size of your love is the amount of pleasure minus the amount of pain.

To illustrate this point, here are five relationship scenarios that you may encounter in your relationships with others:

The Big One:	High pleasure/low pain
A Friend:	Medium pleasure/low pain
Acquaintances	Low pleasure/low pain
Crazy Love	High pleasure/high pain
The Enemy	Low pleasure/high pain

The big fish is the one who contributes consistent, high levels of pleasure and only occasional low levels of pain to your relationship.

DECIDE EXACTLY WHAT YOU WANT

So what do you look for in a man that would clue you in on potential pleasure and pain over time?

> "Boyfriends weren't friends at all; they were prizes, escorts, symbols of achievement, fascinating strangers, the Other."
>
> Susan Allen Toth
> Author of *Blooming*

If you look closely and evaluate wisely, there are some ways to see through the clever disguises of men. Here are some suggestions:

☺ **Start with a winner, not a loser.** A person with winning traits is the only one who will be able to deliver consistent pleasure and very little pain. Remember that all big fish are winners. Don't waste your precious time, energy, and emotion on long-shot losers. Their excuses of bad luck rarely change.

☺ **Monitor your pulse, not your purse.** A Greek proverb reads, "Love can not grow without passion." If a man doesn't drive your passion, you have no chance at the big romance, even if he has a fat wallet. Remember to go for a man who turns you on, not off. There is no substitute for chemistry.

☺ **Aim for character rather than "a character."** Men can be very charming with their manly strengths and boyish personalities. But underneath a man's charm lies a foundation of character. If consistent, lasting, and fulfilling love is your objective, character is one of your only reliable indicators.

☺ **Seek a warm heart, not a cold shoulder.** An undeniable and mysterious part of us seems to be attracted to cool, aloof people. But if you want a relationship with warmth, care, sincerity, and compassion, be sure that the ones you want also possess these vital emotional qualities for love. A man can only give away to you what he possesses inside.

☺ **Find a lifestyle match, not a mismatch.** Even the most charming, attractive and exciting men may not be right for you. If you don't have similar values and lifestyles, differences may start to accumulate, deepen and widen. Remember that opposites may attract initially, but tend to repel over time. In the long-run, similar values and lifestyles create the most secure relationship bonds. Difference may be welcomed in style, but not in substance.

ᦗ **Select a personality complement, not a clash.** There's no denying that everyone enjoys the company of a person with a so-called "good personality." However some personalities will blend better with yours than others. Consistent personality conflict usually means tons of consistent emotional pain. Choose harmony instead of conflict in a loving relationship if you truly want long-term, stable, and consistent happiness.

There is nothing simple about men whether it is trying to catch them or understand them. But an intelligent approach to defining exactly what you want and what you don't want will lead you in the right direction toward love and happiness and away from pain and suffering.

Decide In Advance

Carol Botwin, author of *Tempted Women,* advised, "Pick a man for his qualities, his values, and his compatibility with you, rather than what he represents in status, power or good looks."

The challenge is to make your evaluations early in the relationship, before you get emotionally involved. Otherwise, even the smartest women can end up in the dumbest relationships.

Remember, the secrets to your success in finding an ideal partner are: 1) make intelligent evaluations, 2) concentrate your energies on the right man and the right situation for you, and 3) think long-term.

> "There are games and manipulations to make someone love you and want to marry you, but this doesn't ensure that he or she is right for you."
> John Gray
> Author of *Mars and Venus on a Date*

If you can do that, you will stop wasting time being faked out by the small suitors. That will leave you with more time to focus on what you truly want and need: an attractive man that you like and respect with lots of game and plenty of heart for you.

THE BOTTOM LINE

Men are like fish. Don't let the small ones grab your attention and steal your bait. Concentrate on catching only the bigger ones. You rarely get any better than what you aim for. Be smart, be patient, and aim high.

BIZARRO by Dan Piraro

Excuse me, which brand of instant rice would leave me with the most time to REALLY LISTEN to my partner express her feelings?

AWARD-WINNING SUPERMARKET PICK-UP LINE

www.uexpress.com

Twelve

Fishing Holes

INVEST YOUR TIME IN THE BEST SPOTS

Most of the world is covered by water.
A fisherman's job is simple:
Pick out the best parts.

Charles F. Waterman
Author of *Modern Fresh and Salt Water Fly Fishing* (1975)

fish•ing holes: 1. small areas of a lake, river, or stream where fish congregate or feed. 2. high percentage places for catching fish. 3. where to meet the men you want.

Have you ever found yourself, like the country song says, "looking for love in all the wrong places?"

Dr. Joy Browne, a radio talk-show host and author of *Dating For Dummies*, wrote: "If you're hanging out at Joe's Pub or sitting on your fanny in front of the tube, the perfect date—someone who lights your fire, rings your chimes, or at least doesn't make you nauseous—is gonna remain the stuff of fantasy instead of reality."

If you want to meet the right man for your love life, then you'll have to start looking for love in all the "right" places instead.

MY LOW-PERCENTAGE SINGLES' BAR

For many men and women, the bar scene is a popular and convenient way to meet members of the opposite sex. But like a lot of strategies, there is a smart way and a dumb way to go about it.

A favorite bar of mine is a place called *Panama Joe's Cantina* in Long Beach, California. I had been going there almost every week for the last eight to ten years.

One day it occurred to me that in about a thousand or so visits to *Panama Joe's Cantina*, I'd only met one woman who I had any kind of a dating relationship with.

One in a thousand is not a very good percentage for

meeting people. I would hate to go through another thousand visits in order to find a second date.

> "The best fisherman in the world can't catch
> them if they aren't there."
>
> Anthony Acerrano
> Fishing editor of *Sports Afield*

While the bar scene may be a good place to spend an occasional evening listening to music or watching a sporting event on the big screen, it may not be the most intelligent choice to invest major social energies in the search for your big romance.

When asked on the subject of going to bars to meet first-rate partners, Ann Landers, the syndicated columnist and author of *Wake-up and Smell the Coffee*, wrote, "If you want to catch trout, don't fish in a herring barrel."

In fishing and your love life, always remember that you can't catch the ones you want if they are not where you are.

A SIMPLE FISHING ANALOGY

With today's modern technology, there is an electronic device for locating the position of deep-water fish called a fishfinder.

I was flipping through a fishing magazine when I came across an advertisement that read: "*The ProFish II Fishfinder* brings big-league color fishfinding to the small boat, recreation fisherman. It does it first-class with features that include depth ranges up to 1500 feet, eight-level color signal processing, high-speed zoom, graphical fair-

A third of all romances start on the job.... Office romance is alive and well, despite a barrage of corporate counter-measures.... Between 6 million and 8 million Americans enter into a romance with a fellow employee each year.... About half of all office romances evolve into lasting relationships or marriage.

U.S. News & World Report
December 14, 1998

way guidance screens, car-like speedometer graphics, split screens, turbo-speed plotter redraw and more."

With the aid of a fishfinder, an angler can effectively locate the position of big fish. That way smart anglers can fish in the best places.

In fishing and in your love life, make sure that you invest the majority of your time in the most likely areas for catching the ones you want.

CREATE YOUR OWN OPPORTUNITIES

Dr. Natasha Josefowitz, author of *Paths of Power: A Woman's Guide From First Job to Top Executive*, wrote, "What is luck? It is not only chance, it is also creating the opportunity, recognizing it when it is there, and taking it when it comes."

> "When luck offers a finger one must
> take the whole hand."
> Swedish proverb

To help you get lucky in meeting a "big fish," here are some valuable ideas to factor into your love strategy for men:

- **Go where the big ones are.** Remember that all big fish are winners. If you want to meet a winner, then go to places where winners like to go. Make a study of the type of person you would like to meet and ask yourself, "Where would a man like this tend to go and when would he spend time there?" After you've come up with an answer, make sure to be there.

You can go it alone, but it's a
longer, harder process. I
caution you, however, not to
take on everything by
yourself. You want to
simplify the journey to
having your dream, not
complicate it. The people
you need to help you make
your dream come true are
everywhere, and
within your reach.

Marcia Wieder
Author of *Making Your Dreams Come True*
(1993)

❧ **Go where they are biting**. People are most approachable when they are deeply involved in an activity. Whether the activity is related to sports, entertainment, political causes, education, travel, shopping, friends, family, church, or work, the best way to meet people is getting involved in stimulating activities. You can meet people more naturally around an activity than you can by direct effort.

❧ **Go for some atmosphere**. Standing in a long line at the Department of Motor Vehicles is one of the most unpleasant environments. On the other hand, taking an afternoon stroll along a sandy beach in Maui might put someone in a fabulous mood. Atmosphere is one of the intangibles that has a powerful affect on how well people interact. Look for places that have stimulating or aesthetically pleasing atmospheres to help you meet people in more favorable moods.

❧ **Cultivate your own backyard**. Don't discount the importance of proximity. The "big one" you've been dreaming about may be standing outside in your own backyard. Since the majority of your time is spent where you live or work, the odds are that you'll be more likely to meet people there. We tend to think that someone special will appear in only magical settings. But more often than not, opportunity comes disguised in plain clothes, normal activities, and everyday surroundings.

᭦ **Expand and tap your social networks.** One of the easiest ways to meet people is by referral. Your friends, family, and associates can be your greatest source of social opportunities if you are willing to ask for help. Network marketing companies like Amway, Mary Kay Cosmetics, Excel Communications, and NuSkin are founded on the same principle of people sharing with friends. By learning to expand and tap your social network, you can greatly increase your number to good social opportunities.

᭦ **Try something new and different.** Get away from your routine and the people you normally encounter. Sometimes a healthy break from your regular life may be the stimulus you need to kick-start your love life. The ideal partner for you may be similar in some ways, but unique in other ways. While you are looking for a man with similarities, remember to be equally sensitive to the man who is a little bit different.

᭦ **Take a vacation for faster action.** Vacations are a hotbed for romance. Good bets include: cruises, Club Med villages, ski resorts, tropical destinations, weekend getaways, business trips, and resort seminars. A major drawback to falling in love with someone on vacation is the pain associated with long-distance romances. These love affairs often result in either shattered fantasies or major relocations. But if it's fast action you crave, nothing tops a steamy vacation romance. Just remember to handle it with caution.

A Chinese proverb reads, "Intelligence consists in recognizing opportunity." Get clear on what you want, go to the best meeting places, and engage in the right kinds of activities. Then you will have an easier time recognizing your love opportunities.

INVEST YOUR TIME IN THE BEST SPOTS

Woody Allen, the actor, writer, and filmmaker said, "Eighty percent of success is showing up."

If you want the probabilities to work in your favor, spend the majority of your social time in the best meeting spots for the men you want.

Then when your opportunity for love finally comes around, be sure to pull the trigger and follow through with the appropriate interactions.

> "It doesn't matter how many times you have
> failed. What matters is the successful attempt."
> Dr. Maxwell Maltz
> Author of *The Search for Self-Respect*

Success at meeting the right kind of men for your love life is simply a matter of playing the numbers game more intelligently.

If you want to improve your luck at meeting the man of your dreams, go to the right places and be there more often.

THE BOTTOM LINE

Men are like fish. If you consistently cast an attractive bait into a high-percentage fishing hole, you'll eventually get a good strike from a big fish. Men can rarely resist the temptation of attractive, available bait.

BALLARD STREET Jerry Van Amerongen

Thirteen

The Crowds

Outposition your competition

Even though competition has no place in fly-fishing, and should be none, the angler ought to strive always to play a good game. He should practice the tactics of his art with the same zeal as do the followers of competitive sports if he hopes ever to become an expert fly-fisherman in the highest sense of that much misused term.

George La Branche
Author of *The Dry Fly and Fast Water* (1914)

crowd: 1. a large group of people confined in a restricted area. 2. your competition for catching the big fish. 3. all other women.

If you find yourself in a mountain forest being pursued by an angry grizzly bear, are your chances of escaping better by running uphill or downhill?

The answer is neither. The grizzly bear can easily catch you in either direction.

The best strategy for escaping an angry grizzly bear is to make sure that you bring along a much slower friend.

> "I don't have to be enemies with someone
> to be competitors with them."
> Jackie Joyner-Kersee
> Olympic champion

The point I am trying to make is this: sometimes the difference in life between success and failure is merely a matter of being one up on your immediate competition.

Gelett Burgess, the American illustrator and author (1866-1951), wrote, "Most women have all other women as adversaries; most men have all other men as their allies."

One of the realities of love and life is that competition is a force that has to be reckoned with from time-to-time. This is especially true for women.

A SIMPLE FISHING ANALOGY

According to the *USA Today* April 18, 1997 edition: "44 million people hooked on fishing spend billions...The National Sporting Goods Association ranks fishing with 44.2 million participants in 1995, as the nation's No. 5 favorite activity behind such universal standbys as walking, biking, swimming, and working out on gym equipment."

With the growing popularity of fishing, it's common these days to find the shores of lakes and streams overcrowded with eager anglers.

> "Crowded Waters: There are times when the promise of fast, furious action—and, especially, the promise of big fish—eclipses aesthetic concerns.
>
> Tom Davis
> Author of *The Little Book of Flyfishing*

In order to fish effectively, today's anglers must learn to not only outsmart the fish, but they also must outsmart the other anglers. Otherwise, the angler is more likely to spend the day crossing lines with others instead of catching the big fish.

For success in fishing and in your love life, be sure you know how to deal effectively with crowds.

YOU CAN'T WIN THEM ALL

One winter I went to Idaho for the Annual Sun Valley Singles' Ski Week. On the first night I met a woman named Deanna, who I shared some fun moments with.

The next day I got together with Deanna for a night on the town. As we pulled onto Main Street, we saw a big sign outside of one of the bars that read, "Hot Jeans Contest Tonight."

Deanna said, "I'd like to enter that contest."

We got out of the cab, went inside the bar, and joined the wild crowd. Deanna entered the "Hot Jeans Contest," won her preliminary round, and advanced to the finals.

As the final round was about to begin, the announcer yelled out, "And now, help me bring up our celebrity judge for the final round, Mr. Clint Eastwood."

The crowd roared with approval as Clint took a seat up front with the other judges. Deanna was one of six contestants. When it was over, Deanna had come in a disappointing fifth place.

After the results were announced, Deanna and I were standing around the bar when none other than Clint Eastwood came by. He said to Deanna, "I gave you all the points I could."

Deanna gave Clint a big hug.

I reached out my hand and said, "Hi, Clint. My name is Steve Nakamoto."

He replied, "Whatever."

I stood around for a few minutes before I realized that I was the odd man out on the conversation. I excused myself, thinking that I would hook up with Deanna later in the evening. But that was not to be the case. From that moment on, Clint and Deanna spent the rest of the week together.

I consoled myself with the thought that Deanna must

have had a tough choice: Clint Eastwood (*People Weekly's* 1998 #3 most powerful celebrity) or Steve Nakamoto?

It could have gone either way, right?

> "The strategy to use depends on which rung
> you occupy on the ladder."
> Al Ries and Jack Trout
> Marketing experts

Sometimes competition for the opposite sex is something you have to deal with, whether you like it or not. The most that you can do is give each competition your best shot and let the chips fall where they may. You can't expect to win them all.

OUTPOSITION THE COMPETITION

In their book, *Positioning: The Battle For Your Mind,* business consultants Al Ries and Jack Trout discuss strategies for marketing products or services so they get "positioned" in the forefront of the buyer's mind.

To help position yourself in the forefront of a man's mind, here are some important guidelines to consider:

- ☺ **Be first.** Being first is the simplest way to position yourself ahead of the competition. Those who wait only get what is left. Find out what you want and hustle ahead of the crowd.

- ☺ **Size up your competition.** Battles are more easily won when your strengths are matched up against your rival's weaknesses. Be smart and only compete when the match-ups are more in your favor. Otherwise, don't compete at all.

121

☻ **Be different, be unique.** If you can't be the best in one category, then be the best in another category. You can outshine your competition, for example, by being smarter, kinder, stronger, more confident, more passionate or a better listener. The battle of talents has predictable results: the one with the most talent wins. Shift the playing field onto one of your areas of strengths. Fight your battles there instead.

☻ **Outclass your rivals.** Rise above petty competition. Don't get caught up in putting down your rivals. If you can't compete with class, choose not to compete at all. Maintain your integrity and dignity. The classy manner in which you play the game also gets noticed and appreciated.

☻ **Defend yourself against attackers.** Learn to shield and defend yourself from unfriendly attacks. Realize that some people build themselves up by tearing others down. Don't let them do that to you. If you want others to respect you, be sure to respect yourself by standing firm against unfriendly verbal attacks.

☻ **Make good alliances.** One of the best ways to disarm your rivals is to associate yourself with good friends. Friends can support and protect you from the unkind attacks of rivals. Surround yourself with quality friends to help you protect your backside.

Dealing effectively with competition is about becoming

the best you can be and marketing yourself in the most creative and advantageous ways.

Remember That It Only Takes One

Aristotle Onassis, the Greek financier (1906-1975), said, "The secret of business is to know something that nobody else knows."

Knowing how to "position" effectively will tilt the odds of success in your favor. Even though you may lose an occasional battle, you'll get more than enough chances to come out ahead in the long run.

> "He that wrestles with us strengthens our
> nerves and sharpens our skill.
> Our antagonist is our helper."
> Edmund Burke
> British statesman

While the saying goes, "There are plenty of fish in the sea," in the sport of love, you only need one in order to succeed.

Learn to deal effectively with competition and you will eliminate a major hindrance to your love life.

The Bottom Line

Men are like fish. The big fish attract a larger crowd. Your chances for success lie in establishing the best possible position against your competition.

IN THE BLEACHERS   By Steve Moore

Fish horror stories.

Fourteen

The Cast

Don't scare away men with bad approaches

It is not easy to tell one how to cast.
The art must be acquired by practice.

Charles Orvis
Author of *Fishing with a Fly* (1883)
from
Well-Cast Lines by John Merwin

cast: 1. the act of throwing your fishing line and hook into the water. 2. a well-planned approach to your target fish. 3. how to meet more effectively the men you want.

Letty Cottin Pogrebin, author of *Down With Sexist Upbringing,* wrote, "Boys don't make passes at female smart asses."

If you want men to make a good "pass" at you, develop an effective style of approach. Some women can slip into almost any social situation quickly and easily. However, others are more apt to scare men away with bad or awkward approaches.

You will have no chance of catching any man who has been scared away by your approach.

A SIMPLE FISHING ANALOGY

The word for "approach" in the world of fishing is "cast." Learning to cast properly is the key skill to not scaring away the fish.

> "I wanted to be interested in and knowledgeable
> about one thing. I wanted to learn not to
> frighten a trout in the water."
>
> Gretchen Legler
> Author of *Border Water*

According to the fishing guidebook, *The Curtis Creek Manifesto,* by Sheridan Anderson, "Frightened fish can't be caught! Heavy duty fish frighteners include: vibration, carnivores (if you can see the fish, they can see you), shadows, strange movements—even your tip, other scared fish, a sloppy cast, lunkers, indiscreet pick-up, etc., and so forth. You can't avoid scaring some of the fish, but the less you scare, the more you catch."

In fishing and in your love life, the only fish you can catch are the ones you don't scare away. Be sure your approaches are well-planned and effective.

THE WEEKEND CRUISE TO MEXICO

Every weekend the *M.S. Holiday* sails out of Los Angeles to Ensenada, Mexico. It is a three-day cruise that is filled with good times and a chance to hook-up with a little romance.

Things happen quickly on this cruise. The first night is Get Acquainted Night. The second night is the Captain's Gala Event. And the third night is the Farewell Party. In spite of the short amount of time, people make good friendships, and in some cases, lasting romances.

One of the main reasons people hit it off so well is that there are several easy opportunities to meet people.

> "The best way to meet people is to do what you love to do. Activity is the most natural and comfortable way to make contact."
> Steve Bhaerman and Don McMillan
> Authors of *Friends & Lovers*

You can naturally meet people during the fire boat drill, dancing in the disco, gambling in the casino, dining in the restaurant, grabbing a seat for the show, putting down a tropical cocktail, taking the excursion bus, lounging by the

You can make more friends
in two months by
becoming really interested
in other people, than you
can in two years by trying
to get other people
interested in you. Which is
just another way of saying
that the way to make a
friend is to be one.

Dale Carnegie, Author of
How to Win Friends and Influence People (1936)

pool, playing a game of shuffleboard, walking the decks, or mixing it up at the Singles' Mingle Party.

With a few helpful pointers, almost anyone can have a great time making new friends. It is during these activities that anything can happen, including romance.

The art of approaching people on the *M.S. Holiday* weekend cruise is nothing more than sharing a good time and making a favorable first impression.

We could just as easily take the stress out of meeting new people by using this same casual attitude in our normal day-to-day lives.

MAKE A GOOD FIRST IMPRESSION

A popular American saying goes, "You only get one chance at making a good first impression."

Numerous studies show how in only a few seconds, people clearly decide whether you are a "yes," "no," or "maybe." With this in mind, here are some pointers to help you avoid being an automatic "no" in the minds of the men you want:

- **Be approachable.** Create space and make it inviting for men to meet you. Do your best to give off non-verbal signals that you want to meet and talk with someone. A warm smile on your face is a good place to start.

- **Start with unconscious rapport.** People can create unconscious bonds through non-verbal communication. A word that describes this bonding process is "rapport." Michael Brooks, a communications expert and the author of *Instant Rapport*,

129

Move things off-center with a non-threatening question. The best ice-breaker in this age of everybody moving around is: Where are you from? Geography is the most neutral of subjects, but is pregnant with conversation possibilities. It opens up a whole range of secondary questions, allows you to compare impressions of places where you've been, and prompts you to explain how you come to be where you are. More than that depends on chemistry.

Glen Waggoner and Peggy Maloney
Authors of *Esquire Etiquette* (1987)

wrote: "People primarily experience the world through one of three senses: sight, sound, or feeling. By being aware of a person's gestures, breathing patterns, eye movements, and language, you can pinpoint his or her particular sensory preference. And armed with this knowledge, you can take charge: Match your style—-whether it's visual, auditory, or kinesthetic—-to that of another and become instantly more persuasive, effective, and even lovable."

ⓥ **Break the ice easily.** Find non-threatening topics to get your conversations started quickly and easily. Remind yourself that the best conversations are mostly pleasant in nature. Play it safe by avoiding sensitive subjects like politics, religion, money, and sex. Those kinds of issues can wait until you know the other person a little better.

ⓥ **Show him you care.** A Japanese proverb reads, "One kind word can warm three winter months." People are more interested in how much you care about them, than in how much you know. Show them how much you care by your examples of kindness, sincerity, respect, and compassion.

ⓥ **Remember his name.** Dale Carnegie, author of *How to Win Friends and Influence People*, wrote, "If you remember my name, you pay me a subtle compliment; you indicate that I have made an impression on you. Remember my name and you add to my feelings of importance." Like a warm smile, remembering a person's name is one of the simplest, yet most effective ways to make a good first impression.

⑨ **Avoid the conversation killers.** If you want to keep a conversation alive, don't: criticize, complain, condemn, argue, interrupt, finish other's sentences, put down others, insist on your views, or dwell on negative subjects. Seek areas of agreement rather than areas of disagreement. Save your debates for the political arenas.

⑨ **Get him to play.** If you can get people to laugh at themselves, you can automatically become their friend. Remember that most people are naturally cautious. If you can find creative ways to get them to play or lighten up, you're well on your way to an enjoyable interaction.

⑨ **Disarm him with compliments.** Oscar Wilde, the Irish playwright (1854-1900), wrote, "Women are never disarmed by compliments. Men always are. That is the difference between the sexes." One of the best ways to move a man emotionally is to keep him off-balance with a timely and tasteful compliment. Try either his positive character traits (honesty, sincerity, caring) or his taste in what he wears (neckties), or owns (cars).

⑨ **Make him fear a lost opportunity.** Men absolutely hate or fear the feeling of rejection. Make sure that men know you are available for dating. The best kind of availability, however, is limited availability. If you're never available, men will think you're already involved or not interested. But if you're available all the time, they'll think there must be something wrong with you. The best strategy is to be something in between. Make the man fear a lost opportunity more than being rejected.

To approach others effortlessly or to be comfortably approached by others is the essence of "casting." It is a difficult skill that gets easier with study, practice, feedback, and refinement.

> "Opportunity only knocks once."
>
> English proverb

The important thing to remind yourself when you are casting is that you can only catch the ones that haven't been scared away. Learn to cast effectively and you will have lots of men around to check out your bait.

THE BOTTOM LINE

Men are like fish. They get spooked easily by the slightest negative vibe. Learn not to scare them away by making your first impression nothing less than outstanding.

IN THE BLEACHERS   By Steve Moore

Fifteen

The Snags

Beware of the hidden obstacles

There is not a fly-fisherman on earth,
no matter how skilled, who has not
been humbled by a low-hanging
branch or a submerged boulder.

Judy Muller
Author of "A Woman's Place," *Home Waters: A Fly-Fishing
Anthology,* edited by Gary Soucie (1991)

snags: 1. hidden or unseen obstacles and barriers 2. the negative emotions that keep love away. 3. the illusions of fear and doubt that can be removed entirely by human courage.

In our love lives, we can experience obstacles, whether they are real or imagined, that get in the way of the love we so deeply want and need.

> "Without love our life is...like a ship without a rudder...like a body without a soul."
> Shalom Aleichem
> Russian-born humorist

To prevent this from happening, we must first identify the obstacles and then either avoid or remove them completely from our lives.

What we all want is a clear path to love.

A SIMPLE FISHING ANALOGY

In fishing, a snag is an underwater obstacle, like a sunken tree limb or a large rock, that catches or tangles your fishing line.

Tony Whieldon, author of *The Complete Guide to Fishing Skills*, wrote: "There's always a risk of snagging your line on an underwater obstruction. If you know the position of an obstruction, hold the float back harder than normal so that the hookbait will swing up and over the snag. Having an intimate knowledge of an area suddenly helps you avoid snags. Wear sunglasses, which cut out the surface glare and allow you to see objects more clearly under the water."

In fishing and in your love life, beware of the hidden obstacles. Don't let snags prevent your bait from reaching your desired target.

AVOID THE IMPOSSIBLE OBSTACLES

When I was in high school, I had a crush on a girl named Sue who lived in my neighborhood. Almost every evening she would stop by my house and we would walk her German shepherd around the block together. At first we were just good friends. But before long, we were holding hands and finding secret places to kiss.

My problem was that her father wouldn't let me take her on a date because of his prejudice against my Japanese heritage. At first we tried our best to sneak around him, but eventually the weight of the hassles broke us apart.

> "Every obstacle is for the best."
> Greek proverb

At that young age, there was nothing we could have done to correct the situation. Her father's disapproval of me was an obstacle that should have been avoided completely. But I was only sixteen years old and didn't know any better.

A word to the wise: There are some obstacles, like pursuing married game, that are better off being avoided altogether, rather than challenged.

Be smart. Recognize and avoid impossible situations.

Commit yourself to a
dream: Nobody who tries to
do something great but
fails is a total failure. Why?
Because he can always rest
assured that he succeeded
in life's most important
battle—he defeated
the fear of trying.

Robert H. Schuller, Author of
Tough Times Never Last, But Tough People Do!
(1984)

REMOVE EMOTIONAL OBSTACLES

On the other hand, emotional obstacles, which only exist in your mind, are the hurdles that need to be removed, not avoided. These obstacles only prevent you from taking necessary actions to make love happen.

Until you remove these obstacles, love may avoid you, in spite of your knowledge and skill in other areas of love.

> "Nothing in life is to be feared.
> It is only to be understood."
>
> Marie Curie
> French chemist

To avoid missing out on love, here are some major emotional obstacles to locate and remove from your life entirely:

- **Excessive Frustration.** One of the realities of life is that you don't succeed every time. In some areas, like love, the probabilities can be as high as one in a thousand. Don't let your frustration damage the quality of your attempts. In order to succeed at love, each attempt at love must be optimistic and positive.

- **Fear of Failure.** Marilyn Ferguson, author of *The Aquarian Conspiracy,* wrote, "Ultimately, we know deeply that the other side of every fear is a freedom." Be willing to take a chance. If you want what you truly desire, be sure to aim high. Realize that aiming high means you will occasionally come up short. Don't play it too close to the vest. Go for what you want. Otherwise you'll have to settle for what you don't want.

- ☙ **Fear of Rejection.** If someone says no to your advances, it's either a sign to ask again, ask at another time, ask in another way, or ask someone else instead. Sometimes your best prospects are no more than prospects. Give each opportunity your best shot and if the response is not good move on. If you're not right for them, then they're not right for you.

- ☙ **Lack of Courage.** A Philippine proverb reads, "Courage beats the enemy." You can beat your fears by simply taking decisive action. Don't let your mood at the moment stop you from the action that you know must be taken. Realize that it is often only the first step that is difficult. The rest is usually much easier.

- ☙ **Lack of Faith.** Comete de Buffon, the French naturalist (1707-1788), wrote, "Never think that God's delays are God's denials. Hold on; hold fast; hold out. Patience is genius." You hear a lot about a lack of commitment, but behind this fear is the broader issue of a lack of faith. Faith is simply the absolute knowing that consistent good actions translate into good results. Realize that the rewards can often be delayed and indirect.

Many of these obstacles in their milder forms are simple warnings to prepare for action. But in their "excessive" form, they prevent us from the good actions that we would ordinarily take.

OBSTACLES ARE ONLY ILLUSIONS

Dr. Wayne Dyer, author of *Real Magic* and *The Sky's the Limit*, wrote, "The only block to your happiness is your belief that you have blocks."

The obstacles or blocks that you may sense are only an illusion. When you muster up the courage, decide what you want, take congruent action, and keep persevering, you are removing the imaginary emotional obstacles from your life.

> "A clear understanding of negative emotions
> dismisses them."
>
> Vernon Howard
> Author of *Esoteric Mind Power*

Opportunities for love only become available to you, after you've avoided or removed the snags in your love life.

THE BOTTOM LINE

The obstacles of your love life can be removed by the strength of your character. Don't ever let fear stand in your way of love and happiness. When you are faced with a challenge, resolve to take consistent, decisive action.

SINGLE SLICES   by Peter Kohlsaat

Sixteen

The Nibbles

GAUGE YOUR EARLY RESPONSES WISELY

He that will be an expert angler, must
be endured with the following
qualifications: PATIENCE, DILIGENCE,
and RESOLUTION. Patience to endure
the disappointment that attends
anglers; diligence in observing the
various seasons of the year, and
various dispositions of fish; resolute, to
rise early, and pursue his sport,
whether it be hot or cold,
in winter or summer.

The Angler's Guide (1828)
from
The Angler's Quotation Book by Eric Restall

nib•bles: 1. small or hesitant bites. 2. the early phase of getting to know a man better. 3. a social process commonly known as dating.

An English proverb reads, "Do not judge the size of the ship from the land."

In our love lives, we often try to evaluate the future size of a love relationship based on sketchy first impressions. If we like the first impression, then we are more inclined to take a closer look at the other person so we can make a more accurate judgment. This is a process we commonly call dating.

A SIMPLE FISHING ANALOGY

In fishing, when a fish takes a small bite out of a piece of bait it's called a nibble. Some fish bite lightly, others more firmly, and still others like to grab and run.

Since anglers can rarely see under the water's surface, the best they can do is gauge the quality of the nibble by the strength of the tug on the line.

If an angler fails to gauge the nibble properly, he or she may lose a fish by either overreacting to a weak nibble or not reacting in time to a strong one.

In fishing and in your love life, gauge your early responses wisely so you can respond immediately with the appropriate counteractions.

MY TYPICAL FIRST DATE

My first date with Nora was at Damon's, a Japanese restaurant. It's a fun place by the beach, with rock and roll music, and good seafood.

I ordered teriyaki chicken (the cheapest dinner on the menu) while Nora ordered broiled scallops (one of the most expensive items on the menu).

> "The traditional male-female dynamics is enjoyable. We like doors opened for us and meals paid for on the first date. Otherwise we think he's cheap."
>
> Christina Hoff Sommers
> *Esquire*, February 1994

At the end of the meal, I noticed that Nora hadn't finished three of her scallops. I love scallops. But since it was our first date, I didn't have the nerve to ask her if I could eat them. I didn't want to come across as being cheap. She also ordered two glasses of chardonnay from the wine list at $6.25 a glass. Luckily for me, she didn't order a piece of cheesecake to go.

Dating reveals clues into a person's personality, values, lifestyle, and character. Nora's challenge was to find out whether I regarded her as being worth it or if I was just a cheapskate.

Not being worthy is grounds for ending the dating relationship immediately. Being a cheapskate, while not being a great quality is a far lesser evil.

I've figured out why first dates don't work any better than they do. It's because they take place in restaurants. Women are weird and confused and unhappy about food, and men are weird and confused and unhappy about money, yet off they go, the minute they meet, to where you use money to buy food.

Adair Lara
Author of *Welcome to Earth, Mom* (1992)

GAUGE YOUR DATING RESPONSES

To help you gauge your dating responses wisely, here are a few items worth considering:

- ℘ **Understand the dating game.** Sophia Irene Loeb, author of *Epigrams of Eve,* wrote, "Platonic friendship [is]: The interval between the introduction and the first kiss." It is easy to get faked out by a man's behavior in the early stages of a dating relationship. The man you are trying to gauge accurately and wisely is more clearly revealed over time.

- ℘ **Find enjoyable dating experiences.** Dating is a process of getting to know the other person. You can make the process a lot more fun by having enjoyable dating experiences. It's a great way to get out and enjoy an active lifestyle. Dating reveals tastes, values, character, and lifestyle.

- ℘ **Let things unfold slowly.** A hit song from the 1960's was titled, "You Can't Hurry Love." Be patient and let love happen naturally. There's no need to tell your life story on your first date. If your relationship has any future, there will be plenty of time later. Slowing things down also has the side-benefit of letting passion build up.

- ℘ **Measure the size of a man's heart.** An English proverb reads, "Measure men round the heart." A good measure of a man is the amount of kindness, goodness, warmth, consideration, and sincerity he possesses. These qualities are not created instantly. They are emotional habits that are highly valued in a long-term relationship.

⊕ **Be a good judge of character.** If you want a relationship to last in quality, be sure you select a man who is honest. It is a quality that is disguised by words, but gets revealed by actions. Judge more by what a man does rather than what he says. A good loving relationship is built on a solid foundation of trust.

⊕ **Observe his friends for clues.** A Japanese proverb reads, "When the character of a man is not clear to you, look at his friends." Don't underestimate the power of influence. Observe the habits of a man's friends. Their actions are rarely any different than the one you're dating when his guard is down.

⊕ **Trust your intuition.** Dr. Joyce Brothers, psychologist and author, wrote, "Trust your hunches. Hunches are based on facts filed away just below the conscious level." If you sense that something is wrong, you're probably right. Back off and let time reveal the truth. Make your relationship choices before you get emotionally or sexually involved. It's smarter and easier this way.

By following an intelligent approach to dating, you can stay focused on your main goal of consistent long-term happiness.

KEEP YOUR LIFE BALANCE

Dating can be both joyful and heartbreaking. But most importantly, it is necessary. Dr. Judy Kuriansky, author of *The Complete Idiot's Guide to Dating*, wrote, "Remember to treat dating as simply getting to know a person better."

Intelligent dating requires good judgment. By maintaining a balanced life, you will be in a better position to judge which man is right for you and which man is not.

> "You may be attracted to characteristics in a love partner you later become repelled by."
> Dr. Harold H. Bloomfield, author
> *Love Secrets for a Lasting Relationship*

Unlike your high school days, dating is not an end in itself. As an adult, dating serves as a means to finding someone well-suited for an exciting, fulfilling, and lasting relationship.

Enjoyable dating is simply a more interesting and exciting way to help you do the sorting.

THE BOTTOM LINE

Men are like fish. They are creatures of habit. Only pick men with emotional, mental, relationship, and lifestyle habits you want. Be smart. Watch for clues and avoid the men you don't want or need.

Seamed stockings aren't subtle but they certainly do the job. You shouldn't wear them out when out with someone you're not prepared to sleep with, since their presence is tantamount to saying, "Hi there, big fellow, please rip my clothes off at your earliest opportunity." If you really want your escort paralytic with lust, stop frequently to adjust the seams.

Cynthia Heimel
Author of *Sex Tips for Girls* (1983)

Seventeen

The Strike

SET YOUR HOOK PROPERLY

There is no second chance with an experienced trout. I might trick a six-inch native trout or even a ten-inch stocked trout, but to catch a veteran trout, twelve inches or more, I must be perfect, and I seldom am.

Le Anne Schreiber
Former editor of *The New York Times* Sports Section
from
The Angler's Book of Daily Inspiration by Kevin Nelson

strike: 1. a sudden hit on an angler's fishing line. 2. when a fish snatches the bait. 3. the defining moment when a man is vulnerable to falling in love with you.

Love can strike in an instant. The trouble is you never know when, where, who, or if.

In the movie, *Sleepless in Seattle,* Tom Hanks plays a single parent who struggles with life after his wife's recent passing.

When asked about his love for his late wife, he said, "It was a million tiny things that when you add them all up, it just meant that we were supposed to be together, and I knew it. I knew it the very first time that I touched her. It was like coming home. Only to no home I'd ever known. I was just taking her hand to help her out of the car, and I knew it. It was like magic."

When a man falls in love, there is a defining moment when he suddenly feels the magic and the power of love for a particular woman. Without such a moment, a man remains uncertain and restless about his romance. But with this magic moment, he becomes emotionally hooked on the woman.

For love to last, a clever woman must cultivate these magical moments.

A SIMPLE FISHING ANALOGY

In fishing, a strike is when the fish takes a big hit on the bait of the angler. It is a sudden and decisive action.

152

John M. Cole, author of *Striper: A Story of Fish and Man,* wrote: "The strike is a gift the barracuda keeps for its fisherman and always gives with grace. Even though the fish has been seen, even though impending contact has been announced by the creature itself, the meeting has the jolt of a slap on the shins with a two-by-four, the shock of a kick in the groin. Wham!"

When a fish is about to strike with impact the angler must take advantage of the situation by using a method called "setting the hook." This is done by pulling back on the fishing rod in order to sink the point of the hook into the jaw of the fish.

> "There is a final moment of unyielding patience which, in angling, so often makes the difference between fish and no fish."
> Sparse Grey Hackle
> Author of *Fishless Days, Angling Nights*

Setting the hook prevents the fish from falling off during the difficult landing process. Many fish are lost because of weak hook-ups caused by improperly setting the hook.

In fishing and in your love life, be sure to set the hook properly so your catch doesn't fall off when you're trying to land it.

A PROCESS CALLED ANCHORING

For several years, I enrolled in personal development courses that utilized a therapeutic technique called neurolinguistic programming (NLP). NLP incorporates a light trance hypnosis to rewire the unconscious mind to eliminate fears and accomplish goals.

When you have begun to
establish some loving good
feelings with the new man
in your life, you will want a
way to keep those special
warm feelings from going
away. That is, you will want
to "anchor" those feelings
and make them
available "on call."

Tracy Cabot, Ph.D.
Author of *How to Make a Man Fall in Love
With You* (1984)

One NLP tool is called anchoring. It is a way of intentionally creating stimulus-response patterns in the brain.

Madison Avenue advertisers spend millions of dollars using these same anchoring techniques. For example, when you see a charismatic social icon like Michael Jordan drinking Gatorade, wearing Nike shoes, or eating at McDonald's, your brain makes a natural connection between the good feelings you have toward Michael Jordan and the products he endorses. The transfer of positive feelings from Michael Jordan to the products he endorses causes people to buy.

Anchoring is a way to link the response of powerful emotional feelings to the stimulus of something you see, hear, touch, taste, or smell.

> "A man falls in love through his eyes, a woman through her imagination, and then they both speak of it as an affair of 'the heart.'"
>
> Helen Rowland
> Author of *A Guide to Men*

In your love life, you want to set the hook by anchoring positive feelings to something unique about you. (Examples: your looks, name, voice, scent, touch, skin, hair, kiss, handwriting, gifts, cards, pictures, letters.)

SET YOUR HOOK PROPERLY

To assist you in anchoring or setting the hook, here are some important points to consider:

- **Probe for the vulnerable spots.** A man's greatest desire is to be deeply appreciated. Men want to

I don't like to admit it, but if a girl baited her trap with sex, she'd catch me every time—and it's unlikely this will ever cease to work.

Willie Nelson
American singer
from
The Seven Deadly Sins by Steven Schwartz

be: 1) respected, 2) liked, or 3) attractive to the opposite sex. Striking all three areas is a safe bet. But the area that is most undernourished is likely to create the greatest emotional stir. Find the most vulnerable spot and concentrate your efforts there.

ⓥ **Wait patiently for the right moment.** If you act too early you may frighten the man. If you wait too long the magic moment may pass. Look for a time of heightened emotion, when the moment is at its peak and then make your move.

ⓥ **Don't be afraid to take radical action.** Dave Shiflett, author of *The Casting Call,* wrote, "When a fish bites a fake fly, it is much like a person biting into a sandwich and discovering a staple. He quickly spits it out. We must set the hook between the act of biting and the act of discovery." In order to set the hook in a man, be sure to offer a massive dose of pure pleasure before he gets any hint of possible pain. Otherwise he won't strike.

ⓥ **Set the hook with the right look.** Men tend to be visually-oriented, judging from the success of *Playboy* and *Penthouse* magazines. The way you look, dress, groom, and move your body creates a video in the mind of a man. Be sure yours is a video worth watching repeatedly.

ⓥ **Set the hook with the right sound.** Auditory is the second most dominant sensory channel. The right sound means finding the most appealing volume, pitch, tone, and rhythm in your voice. Like a bad tune on the radio, if you don't sound appealing a man will turn you off. Make sure your volume and tone controls are set for enjoyable listening.

@ **Set the hook with the right touch.** Few things communicate love better than the touch of a lover. Whether it's kissing, holding hands, or stroking a man's hair, touch can be magical when it's in the correct location, with the proper amount of pressure, during the peak emotional moment, and with the right person.

@ **Set the hook with the right words.** American journalist, Marya Mannes, wrote, "All really great lovers are articulate, and verbal seduction is the surest road to actual seduction." If you want to cover all the bases, don't forget to write or say it in words. If you have difficulty finding the right words, go to the local drugstore and check out the greeting card section. A well-chosen card with a handwritten message can leave a lasting impression. Don't let your actions do all your talking. Remember to say or write it in well-chosen words.

Use these ideas to help create your own strategies for hooking more deeply into a man's heart and soul.

DON'T TAMPER WITH THE MAGIC

The methods used by therapists provide insights into a

person's behavior. But you must be on guard against the misuse of these methods.

A few years ago, I went to a Club Med Village where I tried anchoring techniques on fellow vacationers. Since I wasn't adept at performing these techniques, I only accomplished two things: 1) People thought I was weird, and 2) I jinxed myself out of any possible romance.

> "Not only has one to do one's best, one must,
> while doing one's best, remain detached from
> whatever one is trying to achieve."
> Janwillen Van De Wetering
> Author of *The Empty Mirror*

At a critical junction, these techniques may be the difference between success and failure at getting someone to fall in love with you. But for best results, use anchoring techniques sparingly and only when they feel natural to you.

When the chance at a magic moment arrives, be ready to set your hook properly. It is your big chance to secure yourself firmly into the heart and mind of the man you want.

If a man is properly hooked, he is much easier to reel in and land.

THE BOTTOM LINE

You can only expect to land a man who has been properly hooked. Setting the hook properly requires boldness, timing, and precision.

REAL LIFE ADVENTURES by Gary Wise and Lance Aldrich

A man finally gets married when all the buttons have
fallen off every piece of clothing he owns.

Eighteen

The Landing

PLAY YOUR CATCH INTO THE NET

It's not a fish until it is on the bank.

Irish Proverb
from
The Fisherman's Guide to Life by Criswell Freeman

land•ing: 1. the process of bringing a hooked fish out of the water and either onto land, inside a boat, or into a net. 2. the process of bringing a man out of the single world and into a committed relationship. 3. the trickiest part of catching a man.

Some of the most exciting and wonderful romances can fall apart before they reach the commitment or marriage stage.

For example, a few years ago actor Brad Pitt and actress Gwyneth Paltrow were a hot item in the news. You may recall when nude pictures of the couple as they vacationed on the island of St. Barts were circulated on the Internet and printed in the tabloids. Under the close eye of the media, their engagement eventually broke off before they made it to the altar.

> "Venus plays tricks on lovers with her game of images which never satisfy."
>
> Lucretius
> Roman philosopher and poet

Romance is a beautiful part of a new relationship. But real love must also pass the tests of time and adversity. After an exciting phase of romance, love must eventually find its way to emotional commitment.

A love is not love until it rests safely in the net of commitment.

A Simple Fishing Analogy

The process of landing a fish is one of the most difficult phases of fishing.

Mike Toth, author of *The Complete Idiot's Guide to Fishing Basics*, wrote: "There are many ways to get a fish out of the water (called 'landing' the fish). However, this is when most fish are lost, because, basically, fish do not want to come out of the water. Even tired or "played out" fish can put forth a burst of energy and try to get away from the angler. Given other factors at this time—-a short line, an excited angler, possibly a rocking boat—-it's not surprising that many fish succeed in escaping."

> "The end of fishing is not angling, but catching."
> Thomas Fuller
> English author

In fishing and in your love life, you must learn how to land effectively. Even the best strikes can be lost to time and adversity.

A Long-Distance Romance

There was a man named Bill and a woman named Janet who met and fell in love at the Club Med Village in Cancun.

During their week together, they had the time of their lives: swimming in the crystal clear waters, dancing in the disco, taking shopping trips into town, and strolling on the beach in the evenings.

I remember seeing them with tears in their eyes as they said good-bye to each other at the airport.

Smart women know the difference between playing hard to get and being hard to get.... Acting as though you're not that interested in him and actively pursing your own interests.

Steven Carter and Julia Sokol
Authors of *What Smart Women Know* (1990)

It turns out that Janet was going back to her life as a housewife with three children and a husband. Bill was going back to the big city and his lifestyle as a single bachelor.

What eventually happened was this: Janet and Bill had another rendezvous. Janet wanted to leave her husband to be with Bill. Bill was uneasy about having an instant family with three children. Janet divorced her husband. But after a few months, Bill painfully abandoned Janet. Janet was left devastated and disillusioned.

> "Love does not consist in gazing at each other but in looking together in the same direction."
> Antoine De Saint-Exupery
> French author

In the final analysis, Janet hooked Bill. But she was unable to land him. There is no denying that hooking is the most thrilling part of the fishing for love process. But without properly landing a romance it remains only a thrill.

PLAY YOUR CATCH INTO THE NET

An Angler's Dictionary by Henry Beard and Roy McKie defines a "net" as a "woven mesh bag attached to a circular wood or metal frame on which a handle is mounted, used to remove hooked fish from the water."

To help you get your romance out of the competitive social waters and into the net of commitment, here are a few items worth considering:

    ⎅ **Factor in the current.** The current works in two

ways. First, the current of good fortune can flow in your direction and make catching too easy. In this case, you have a romance that hasn't tested the strength of your hook-up. Secondly, the current can work against you and make catching extremely difficult. In this case patience and flexibility will help you withstand adversity. Expect frustration, anger, disappointment, and hurt when the current is going against you.

☙ **Don't let tension break your line.** Just as too much pressure can cause a fishing line to break, too much fighting can break-off a relationship. Understand that upsets are simply when someone violates a standard that you have. If your relationship is to survive you must learn to compromise and understand each other. Finding solutions rather than dwelling on problems can be the difference between love or no love. A love ends when you reach the point of irreconcilable differences.

☙ **Play out the fish.** To play in your love relationship means: give and take, tease and be teased, intensity and calm, hot and cold, togetherness and space. A man isn't ready to settle down and commit until after he's gotten a good share of his thrills out. Let the man play himself out, otherwise he'll fight or resist you all the way in.

☙ **Reset the hooks with the promise of great sex.** Whether you engage in sex or not, the promise of an inspiring sexual future is the man's motivation to continue the chase after the woman. But be very careful here. Bad sex in the beginning can bring an immediate end to your future plans. On the other hand, the images of great sex can move emotional mountains.

◎ **Remember to reel him in.** In reasonable time and after a man has been played out, it's time to reel him in. How much time that is depends on your own situation. But when there's no more to be explored as a dating couple, it's time to move forward in your relationship and most importantly, in your life. Sometimes the most wonderful romances can go no further. Without the prospect for growth, love dies. Eventually there comes a time when you either reel him in or cut him loose.

◎ **Ease him into the net.** Mother Teresa said, "Joy is a net of love by which you can catch souls." You may have to withstand a man's last-minute surge to escape to freedom. This can best be handled with calm assurances rather than demanding pressure. Make commitment easy by painting the future with happiness, excitement, joy, and peace of mind.

Follow these guidelines and you will have an excellent chance of landing even the most challenging men.

A good woman
inspires a man.

A brilliant woman
interests him.

A beautiful woman
fascinates him.

A sympathetic woman
gets him.

Helen Rowland
Author of *A Guide to Men* (1922)

That's How The Big One Got Big

William Shakespeare (1564-1616) wrote, "The trout must be caught with tickling."

In a similar way, a man is not caught by external force; he is captured by internal persuasion.

Some of the most attractive, fascinating, and worthwhile men are very difficult to catch because of their fear of commitment or their belief that something better awaits them.

The only women who can catch these game creatures are those who: 1) thoroughly understand the "men are like fish" principles, 2) possess both unyielding patience and unstoppable persistence, and 3) act with boldness and precision at the most opportune moments.

> "Man begins by making love and ends by loving a woman; woman begins by loving a man and ends by loving love."
> Remy De Gourmont
> French novelist and critic

As you've been told throughout this book, cleverness, not beauty, is the ultimate secret to hooking and landing the love you want.

The Bottom Line

Men are like fish. A man is not caught until he is actually landed safely in the net of emotional, rather than verbal commitment. Play your man out and expect a good fight on the way in. Just like a trout, a man must be caught with tickling, not external force.

Nineteen

Catch & Release

DON'T KILL THE ROMANCE

A good game fish is too valuable
to be caught only once.

Lee Wulff
Author of *Trout on a Fly* (1990)

catch & re•lease: 1. a common practice in the sport of fly-fishing, where the angler sets free a fish unharmed immediately after capture. 2. giving a man enough space to periodically and continuously pursue a woman he desires. 3. the secret to keeping romance alive.

A French proverb reads, "Love makes time pass; time makes love pass."

We all want a great love life, one that is exciting, compelling, passionate, fulfilling, and lasting. But this rare combination is hard to find.

> "The secret of staying in love is learning how to make love all the time."
> Barbara DeAngelis, Ph.D.
> Author of *Real Moments for Lovers*

If we truly want happiness out of our love lives, we must seek the thrills of romance while nurturing what it takes to make love grow and last.

MY FLOWER SHOP CUSTOMERS

For years, I worked in my family's flower shop business. Some of our best customers were the men who were actively dating. These fellows would typically come in once or twice a week to buy a dozen long-stem red roses for their dates. In time, some men would put in a big order with us for their wedding. But after the wedding, many of these men would practically disappear.

The only time we would see them again was on Valentine's Day. If they ever returned to our shop as regulars, it would be because they were divorced and actively dating again. It was a sad, but often true commentary on how romance tends to fade away over time.

> "It is absurd to say that a man can't love one woman all the time as it is to say that a violinist needs several violins to play the same piece of music."
>
> Honore de Balzac
> French author

The big romance that stays exciting, grows, and lasts is more the exception than the norm for many people today. Why that is so remains largely a mystery.

A SIMPLE FISHING ANALOGY

In fishing, there is a term that is commonly used called "catch and release." This involves removing the hook from the mouth of the fish and letting it swim away to freedom. Sometimes after a bitter struggle, a fish has to be revived before it can be safely released.

According to the *USA Today* February 17, 1999 edition, "Catch and release [is] catching on.... A recent survey said 58% of all anglers practice the catch-and-release fishing method to preserve fish for future generations."

Sheridan Anderson, author of *The Curtis Creek Manifesto,* wrote, "Releasing: Hold gently until the fish can swim away. Don't injure when landing. Catch and release is the only way to insure the quality of the sport."

Love doesn't just sit there
like a stone, it has to be
made, like bread; remade
all the time, made new.

Ursula K. Le Guin
Author of *The Lathe of Heaven* (1997)

A fish that had been caught and released is available to be caught again.

In fishing and in your love life, catching and releasing is the secret to keeping what you treasure alive and well.

IF YOU LOVE SOMEBODY SET THEM FREE

If it is life-long romance that you desire, don't kill it off by turning it into one of your prized possessions. Set your love free and enjoy the continual process of chasing and catching over and over again.

Grammy Award-winning recording artist Sting said much the same when he wrote and sang, "If you love somebody, set them free."

> "The way to love anything is to realize that
> it might be lost."
>
> G. K. Chesterton
> English author

To prevent your romance from coming to an emotional dead end, here are some ideas to help keep it alive and healthy:

- Create space in your relationship. An English proverb reads, "Familiarity breeds contempt." For love to work, maintain a little bit of breathing room. Don't strive to have everything in common. Maintain some of your personal identity, personal interests, and personal friends. A strong relationship is the sum of two vital individuals. Nourish your individuality while you are simultaneously nourishing your relationship.

- **Never break the trust.** A Swedish proverb reads, "What a moment broke may take years to mend." Don't break the trust in a relationship by being careless in the moment. Once trust is broken it can never return to its original condition. Keep the magic in your romance alive by never crossing the line of trust.

- **Repair with forgiveness.** The only way to fix the past is through total forgiveness. A French proverb reads, "To understand is to forgive." If someone does something wrong unintentionally or unwisely, the only thing you can do to save your relationship is to show your understanding by forgiving the other person.

- **Create and develop new channels for growth.** Like a healthy green plant, a love relationship is either growing or dying. There are no in-betweens. Keep your romance alive by discovering new ways of enjoying and appreciating the wonder of life together.

- **Treasure your moments.** There may come a time in your life when all you have are your memories. Don't take love for granted. Don't wait until you lose it in order to appreciate it. Value your love life and your lover now. Remember how quickly time flies.

Keeping a romance alive and well is no easy task. By following these few simple guidelines and staying committed to your relationship, you will be able to handle most relationship problems in advance.

KEEP THE MAN CHASING

There's an old saying that goes, "A man quits running after he's caught the bus." For a man to stay romantic, a clever woman knows that a small dose of uncertainty keeps a man running after your bus.

A man is wired to chase, pursue, conquer, achieve, and succeed. Don't try to take that basic instinct away from him. If you do, he may either die emotionally or chase after another woman.

> "Pursuit and seduction are the essence of sexuality. It's part of the sizzle."
> Camille Paglia, author
> *Sex, Art, and American Culture*

A Spanish proverb reads, "Take hold lightly; let go lightly. This is one of the great secrets of felicity in love."

A keeper in a love relationship is not someone you hold as a possession to lock up and throw away the key. Instead, a keeper is the one you let go but keeps coming back to you for more.

THE BOTTOM LINE

Men are like fish. If you catch them, they die. If you release them and keep them alive, they are free to regroup and happily chase after you over and over again.

There is a love that begins
in the head, and goes down
to the heart, and grows
slowly; but it lasts till death,
and asks less than it gives.
There is another love, that
blots out wisdom, that is
sweet with the sweetness
of life and bitter with the
bitterness of death, lasting
for an hour; but it is worth
having lived a whole life
for that hour.

Ralph Iron
Author of *The Story of an African Farm* (1883)

Twenty

The Keeper

ENJOY THE JOURNEY

When I have made a difficult cast and
landed it the way I wanted, or fished
over a difficult fish and finally
caught it, I feel true reward.

Jennifer Smith
Author of *Paul Bunyan:*
My Wooly Bugger Chuckling Machine
from
The Angler's Book of Daily Inspiration by Kevin Nelson

keep•er: 1. a big fish worth taking home with pride. 2. a man who contributes massive, consistent, and secure happiness to your life. 3. the love every woman wants and needs.

Here are the final words of the last song ever recorded by the greatest musical group of all-time (according to the 1998 VH1 Poll of Musical Artists), the Beatles, from a song appropriately titled, "The End":

> And in the end...
> The love you take
> Is equal to the love...
> You make.

A clever woman never leaves her love life entirely to luck. Instead, she chooses the path of physical, mental, and emotional preparation.

As a final checklist for making love happen, always remember to:

- ☺ Start with a fresh attitude
- ☺ Maximize your physical talents
- ☺ Increase your ability to play the game
- ☺ Develop more emotional heart
- ☺ Play the percentages in your favor
- ☺ Take feedback and make adjustments
- ☺ Never give up

Naturally, there are some women who might be inclined to say something like, "Men hardly seem worth the trouble. I can live without them. Why should I go through all the hassle?"

After all, Gloria Steinem, the noted American feminist and author, said, "A woman without a man is like a fish without a bicycle."

My best reply is that love preparation is not only about getting a man. Love preparation has a lot to do with learning about people and participating fully in the adventure of life.

ENJOY THE JOURNEY

The final message of this book is:

> Love is a journey, not a destination.
> So most of all, enjoy the journey.

Getting the love you want is only the frosting on the cake. Becoming the special kind of soul who deserves love by giving away love is a far greater and lasting value.

> "Love is never lost. If not reciprocated, it will
> flow back and soften and purify the heart."
> Washington Irving,
> American essayist

When you come to the end of your life, there will be more to treasure than a collection of old photographs and love letters. You will also possess the eternal heart of a loving person.

IF I HAD MY LIFE TO LIVE OVER....

I'd dare to make mistakes next
time. I'd relax. I would limber up.
I would be sillier than I have been
this trip. I would take fewer things
seriously. I would take more
chances. I would take more trips.
I would climb more mountains,
and swim more rivers. I would eat
more ice cream and less beans.

I would perhaps have more actual
troubles but I'd have fewer
imaginary ones. You see, I'm one of
those people who live sensibly and
sanely hour after hour,
day after day.

Oh, I've had my moments and if
I had it to do over again, I'd have
more of them. In fact, I'd try to
have nothing else. Just moments.
One after another, instead of living
so many years ahead of each day.

Nadine Stair
Age 85

A popular saying goes, "You can't take it with you." No words are more true when it comes to the endless acquiring of physical possessions. But the one thing that you can take with you, however, is love.

THE KEEPER IS LOVE

Elbert G. Hubbard, the American author (1856-1915), wrote, "The love you give away is the only love we keep."

Unlike fishing for fish, there are very few "keepers" in life. One of those, however, is love. It is a treasure for eternity, not to be missed for any reason.

Over the course of a person's entire life there are no real excuses for missing out on love, except for the illusions of fear and self-doubt. It is my hope that this book has done a lot to reduce or eliminate these illusions entirely from your life.

> "What we have once enjoyed we can never lose.
> All that we love deeply becomes a part of us."
> Helen Keller

You now possess all you need to catch the big romance and bring it home for keeps. If you get on and stay on the path of love mastery as I have presented in this book there's nothing stopping you from becoming simply irresistible and acquiring the happiness you deserve.

Please go out and make love happen.

We, the fish, are getting tired of swimming around aimlessly. Our true destiny is to be caught by your true love.

Good luck and God bless.

References

Adams, Abby. *An Uncommon Scold.* New York: Fireside, 1994.

Anderson, Sheridan. *The Curtis Creek Manifesto: A Fully Illustrated Guide to the Strategy, Finesse, Tactics and Paraphernalia of Fly-Fishing.* Portland: Frank Amato Publications, 1978.

Beard, Henry and Roy McKie. *Fishing: An Angler's Dictionary.* New York: Workman Publishing, 1983.

Beck, Cathy. *Cathy Beck's Fly-Fishing Handbook.* New York: Lyons & Burford, 1996.

Bhaerman, Steve and Don McMillan. *Friends & Lovers: How to Meet the People You Want to Meet.* Cincinnati: Writer's Digest Books, 1986.

Bignami, Louis and Robert Jones, William R. Rooney, Joel Vance. *Wit & Wisdom of Fishing.* Lincolnwood: Publications International, Ltd., 1998.

Bloomfield, Harold H. and Natasha Josefowitz. *Love Secrets for a Lasting Relationship.* New York: Bantam Books, 1992.

Brooks, Michael. *Instant Rapport: The NLP Program That Creates Intimacy, Persuasiveness, Power!* New York: Warner Books, 1989.

Browne, Joy. *Dating for Dummies.* Foster City: IDG Books Worldwide, Inc., 1997.

Buscaglia, Leo. *Love: A Warm and Wonderful Book about the Largest Experience In Life.* New York: Fawcett Crest, 1985.

Cabot, Tracy. *How to Make a Man Fall in Love with You.* New York: Dell Publishing, 1984.

Carnegie, Dale. *How to Win Friends and Influence People.* New York: Simon and Shuster, 1981.

Carrington, Raye. *Hooked: Witty Quotes from Serious Anglers.* Kansas City: Andrews and McMeel Publishing, 1998.

Carter, Steven and Julia Sokol. *What Smart Women Know.* New York: M. Evans and Co., Inc., 1990.

Davis, Tom. *The Little Book of Fly-fishing.* Minocqua: Willow Creek Press, 1997.

Davis, Wynn. *The Best of Success: a Treasury of Success Ideas.* Lombard: Great Quotations Publishing Company, 1988.

DeAngelis, Barbara. *How to Make Love All the Time.* New York: Dell Publishing, 1987.

Fenchuk, Gary W. *Timeless Wisdom.* Richmond Cake Eaters, Inc., 1995.

Freeman, Criswell. *The Fisherman's Guide to Life: Nine Timeless Principles Based on the Lessons of Fishing.* Nashville: Walnut Grove Press, 1996.

Gray, John. *Mars and Venus on a Date: A Guide for Navigating the 5 Stages of Dating to Create a Loving and Lasting Relationship.* New York: HarperCollins Publishers, Inc., 1997.

Hardy, Ian and Gretchen Zufall. *Screen Kisses: Quotes of Love, Sex, and Romance from the Movies.* New York: Perigee Books, 1997.

Kaminsky, Peter. *Fishing for Dummies.* Foster City: IDG Books Worldwide, Inc., 1997.

Kirby, Mary. *Mary Kirby's Guide to Meeting Men.* New York: McGraw-Hill Book Company, 1983.

Kugach, Gene. *Fishing Basics: the Complete Illustrated Guide.* Harrisburg: Stackpole Books, 1993.

Kuriansky, Judy. *The Complete Idiot's Guide to Dating.* New York: Alpha Books, 1996.

Lakoff, George and Mark Johnson. *Metaphors We Live By.* Chicago: The University of Chicago Press, 1980.

Linfield, Jordan L. and Joseph Krevisky. *Words of Love: Romantic Quotations from Plato to Madonna.* New York: Random House, 1997.

Maggio, Rosalie. *The New Beacon Book of Quotations by Women.* Boston: Beacon Press, 1996.

McKnight, Thomas W. and Robert H. Phillips. *Love Tactics: How to Win the One You Want.* Garden City Park: Avery Publishing Group, Inc., 1988.

Merwin, John. *Well-Cast Lines: The Fisherman's Quotation Book.* New York: Fireside, 1995.

Mieder, Wolfgang. *Illuminating Wit, Inspiring Wisdom.* Paramus: Prentice Hall Press, 1998.

Nelson, Kevin. *The Angler's Book of Daily Inspiration: a Year of Motivation, Revelation, and Instruction.* Chicago: Contempory Books, 1997.

People Entertainment Almanac. New York: People Books, 1998.

REFERENCES

Phillips, Bob. *Phillips' Book of Great Thoughts and Funny Sayings.* Wheaton: Tyndale House Publishers, Inc., 1993.

The Quotable Woman. Philadelphia: Running Press, 1991.

Restall, Eric. *The Angler's Quotation Book.* London: Robert Hale Limited, 1993.

Ries, Al and Jack Trout. *The 22 Immutable Laws of Marketing.* New York: HarperCollins Books, 1993.

Robbins, Anthony. *Awaken the Giant Within: How to Take Immediate Control of Your Mental, Emotional, Physical & Financial Destiny!* New York: Summit Books, 1991.

Rohn, Jim; *Seven Strategies for Wealth and Happiness.* Rocklin: Prima Publishing & Communications, 1986.

Safire, William and Leonard Safir. *Good Advice.* New Jersey: Wings Books, 1982.

Safire, William and Leonard Safir. *Words of Wisdom: More Good Advice.* New York: Fireside, 1989.

Schwartz, Steven. *The Seven Deadly Sins.* New York: Macmillan Publishing, 1997.

Toth, Mike. *The Complete Idiot's Guide to Fishing Basics.* New York: Alpha Books, 1997.

Whieldon, Tony. *The Complete Guide to Fishing Skills.* New Jersey: Crescent Books, 1997.

Wieder, Marcia. *Making Dreams Come True.* New York: Mastermedia Limited, 1993.

Permissions

Single Slices "So how's it going...." cartoon on p. 142: Cartoon by Peter Kohlsaat. Copyright, 1998, Los Angeles Times Syndicate. Reprinted by permission.

Single Slices "I'm no longer the poor little surfer...." cartoon on p. 56: Cartoon by Peter Kohlsaat. Copyright, 1998, Los Angeles Times Syndicate. Reprinted by permission.

Single Slices "and then I got accepted to Dental Hygiene School...." cartoon on p. 142: Cartoon by Peter Kohlsaat. Copyright, 1998, Los Angeles Times Syndicate. Reprinted by permission.

Non Sequitur "I don't want to nit-pick, Doctor, but...." cartoon on p. 30: Cartoon by Wiley Miller. _ 1998, Washington Post Writers Group. Reprinted by permission.

Non Sequitur "My client would like to buy your client...." cartoon on p. 48: Cartoon by Wiley Miller. © 1998, Washington Post Writers Group. Reprinted by permission.

Non Sequitur "Tunnel of love...." cartoon on p. 170: Cartoon by Wiley Miller. © 1998, Washington Post Writers Group. Reprinted by permission.

I Need Help "I'm so upset that Don doesn't trust...." cartoon on p. 90: Cartoon by Vic Lee. © 1998, King Features Syndicate. Reprinted by permission.

In the Bleachers "Stinkin' snag!...." cartoon on p. 134: Cartoon by Steve Moore. © 1998, Universal Press Syndicate. Reprinted by permission.

In the Bleachers "....Jimmy bit. A steel hook pierced his lip..." cartoon on p. 124: Cartoon by Steve Moore. © 1998, Universal Press Syndicate. Reprinted by permission.

In the Bleachers "I can see swallowing the hook...." cartoon on p. 14: Cartoon by Steve Moore. © 1998, Universal Press Syndicate. Reprinted by permission.

Quality Time "Handsome male, loyal, attentive, fun-loving...." cartoon on p. 98: Cartoon by Gail Machlis. © 1998, Universal Press Syndicate. Reprinted by permission.

Bizarro "Excuse me, which brand of instant rice...." cartoon on p. 106: Cartoon Dan Piraro. © 1998, Universal Press Syndicate. Reprinted by permission.

Quality Time "Well, you know how women are...." cartoon on p. 72: Cartoon by Gail Machlis. © 1998, Universal Press Syndicate. Reprinted by permission.

Real Life Adventures I love you. I love you too...." cartoon on p. 160: Cartoon by Wise and Aldrich. © 1998, Universal Press Syndicate. Reprinted by permission.

Ballard Street "Occasionally, you tie into a big one." cartoon on p. 40: Cartoon by Jerry Van Amerongen. © 1998, Creators Syndicate. Reprinted by permission.

Ballard Street "Vavoom!" cartoon on p. 116: Cartoon by Jerry Van Amerongen. © 1998, Creators Syndicate. Reprinted by permission.

Index

The Author

According to Cyndi Haynes and Dale Edwards, the authors of *2002 Ways to Find, Attract and Keep a Mate,* "The Ten Best Occupations for Meeting People from all Backgrounds are doctors, journalists, tour guides, police officers, realtors, flight attendents, hairstylists, florists, retail salespeople, and car salespeople."

Steve Nakamoto is a professional tour director who gets paid to take people on vacation. With more than 27 cruises, 28 Club Med vacations, 10 Singles' Ski Weeks, and over eighty vacation tours, Steve has had a lot of first-hand experience in meeting people of all backgrounds.

Steve's previous experience as a personal development instructor for two leading corporate training groups, along with managing his family's florist business, helped create his unique perspective on love and life.

An avid beach volleyball player and surfer, Steve currently lives in Southern California.

Order Information

Let your friends in on this unique approach to love with their own copy of *MEN ARE LIKE FISH*

CALL TOLL-FREE: (800) 431-1579

Fax orders: (714) 846-0622. Send this form.

E-mail orders: menarelikefish@mindspring.com

Postal orders: Java Books, 17202 Corbina Lane, Suite 204, Huntington Beach, California 92649

Please send _____ copies @ $14.95 each   _____

CA residents add $1.16 sales tax per book   _____

Shipping and handling at $3.00 per book   _____

TOTAL   _____

PLEASE PRINT

Name: _____

Address: _____

City: _____

State:_____

Zip _____

Phone:(___) _____(if we need to contact you about order)

Card number: _____

Name on card: _____

Expiration date:_____Signature: _____

Payment by check: Make payable to **Java Books.**